LOVE **POTIONS**

MAGICKAL (AND EASY!) RECIPES
TO FIND YOUR PERSON,
IGNITE PASSION, AND
GET OVER YOUR EX

VALERIA RUELAS

HEARST
books

This book is dedicated to
my heroes, my mother, sister,
and father for being the best
family a girl could ask for
and to Santa Muerte,
my angel and protector
who opened up the road
to writing this book.

CONTENTS

CHAPTER 1

WELCOME TO BRUJERIA

Bienvenidos al mundo de la brujeria del amor, welcome to the world of love witchcraft! My name is Valeria Ruelas, but most people know me as "The Mexican Witch." I am a professional *bruja*, spiritual teacher, and intuitive tarot reader. For those not familiar, *bruja* is the Spanish word for witch, and *brujeria* is the specific type of witchcraft practiced by the people of Latin America, Spain, and the Caribbean. Brujeria is a sacred art, and is often taught through family lines. If you have no familial ties to brujeria and would like to learn more about it on your own, be mindful to learn from the right teachers.

Out of respect, a person of non-Latino heritage should not refer to themselves as a bruja because a connection to brujeria must be established by blood and culture. However, someone who respectfully learns the art of brujeria can certainly call themselves a witch. Over the past few years, brujeria and witchcraft have become very popular spiritual practices because they bring desires into reality. While the enthusiasm surrounding these topics is very exciting, much of brujeria remains misunderstood. For example, a quick internet search on brujeria will lead you down a rabbit hole to pages of dark and violent images. This is very misleading because, at the core, brujeria and witchcraft are healing arts. As a bruja, I want to teach people the positive sides of witchcraft and brujeria and how they can help you change your life.

TV series like *Chilling Adventures of Sabrina* starring Kiernan Shipka on Netflix and the CW's *Charmed* have also really helped bring witches into the public eye. While publicity is appreciated, these dramatizations can make people believe several misconceptions about what it means to be a real witch. Actual witchcraft is very practical (sorry, we don't create sparks of light or raise people from the dead), and there is nothing inherently frightening about the practice of witchcraft. Real witches who walk among us are normal people just like yourself. They can be healers, feminists, as well as an integral part of your community. In an article in *Newsweek*, Benjamin Fearnow noted that "several recent studies indicated there may be at least 1.5 million witches across the country." He also notes that "With 1.5 million potential practicing witches across the U.S., witchcraft has more followers than the 1.4 million mainline members of the Presbyterian church." This is an astounding number, and it is growing fast![1]

1 https://www.newsweek.com/witchcraft-wiccans-mysticism-astrology-witches-millennials-pagans-religion-1221019

I consider myself an expert in the type of witchcraft I call "botanica magick." This type of magick is simple in many ways but it is also considered to be VERY powerful, involving skills like making magickal herbal oils, candle rituals, and spiritual petitions. I grew up around brujeria and botanicas. My *bis-abuela* (great-grandmother) Maria Luisa was well-known for her practice as a *curandera*, or a healer, in our hometown. People sought her out for psychic advice, energy cleansing, and indigenous medicine. She was renowned for being a powerful healer of the evil eye, and could cure this ailment using only an egg. In many cultures, it is believed that someone can cast an "evil eye" on you if they are jealous or negative. We are all vulnerable to this on an energetic level, and so if we feel negative energy, it is important to release it with the help of a spiritual practitioner.

Generally, in Mexico, people who practice witchcraft are considered healers and spiritual workers. They are sought out for their intuition, ancestral work, and knowledge of practical magick. You can find brujas at stores called *mercados* and *botanicas*, which specialize in selling esoteric supplies and herbal remedies. Lining the walls of these shops are hundreds of colorful glass candles, statues of saints, crystals, bath soaps, and spiritual washes.

My magickal practice is highly inspired by my great-grandmother and our family lineage, but as a modern practitioner of the craft, I find that it is also important to reinvent and get creative with recipes so they don't seem outdated.

By the time you finish reading this book, you will have all the essential knowledge and skills to become a practical witch. You will learn how to do many basic types of spells and create potions that you can use in your daily life for highly effective magick.

THE BASICS OF MAGICK

In witchcraft, *magick* is spelled with a *k* to differentiate it from stage magic (in magick, rabbits aren't being pulled out of hats). Among the many definitions of magick, one of my favorites comes from the renowned occultist Aleister Crowley. He states, "Magick is the science and art of causing change to occur in conformity with will." I like this definition because it is simple to understand and it defines magick as a sort of science.

Although there hasn't been a scientific study to prove that magick is "real," there is no denying the power of manifestation. Think about the placebo effect in clinical trials, when a patient experiences improvement to their health even though they have blindly received a placebo (a fake form of treatment) or a sugar pill. These benefits are due to the patient's blind faith in the treatment that they believe they are receiving, which proves that our thoughts are capable of healing us and affecting our reality.

This is why I like to frame magick as the "use of personal energy" when I explain its effectiveness to skeptics. Intention, love, and faith produce results in magick. The amazing thing about adding magick and ritual practice into your life is that it will amplify the effects of your positive thoughts. Those of us who choose to believe and practice magick are giving our natural powers of attraction a huge energy boost.

SO HOW DO I GET STARTED?

Decide on your purpose and intention, then dedicate time to performing a ritual with the potions you learn from this book. There is no right or wrong way to perform a ritual, but a spell is more likely to succeed if you take the time to plan and meditate on your desired outcome. I suggest that you track your progress in a notebook or spell-work journal when you first begin practicing.

Initially, spell work may seem very mechanical, but as you master your magickal skills your intuition will guide you and magick will become more natural. So that you don't rush the process, plan to work on your spells when you have plenty of time to do so. Be persistent and make sure to continue your energy work through meditation until you achieve your wanted result. It can take a few weeks or sometimes even months, but don't give up.

I recommend that you practice an attraction meditation for ten minutes every morning right after you wake up, and for ten minutes at night, right before you go to bed. Visualize your desired outcome and ask the universe for your magick to work.

THE ESSENTIALS OF MAGICK

In addition to meditation, there are other elements of magick that are critical for achieving results. If you follow these basic rules of magick and manifestation in every ritual you perform, your spell work is guaranteed to have more success.

Opening and Closing

It is very important to come up with a personal way to open and close every ritual you perform. A simple way to do this is by meditating and creating a personal affirmation or prayer to call in your higher self and spiritual guides. Spiritual guides are the energies of bigger forces that accompany and surround you. I usually recommend for beginner witches to only call upon energies that feel familiar and approachable. I often call upon Mother Nature, my benevolent ancestors, and the universe. Envision a white protective light around your sacred space and then say this prayer aloud.

OPENING: "I (insert your full name) summon in the power of my higher self and my spiritual guides to aid and protect me during this sacred ritual."

CLOSING: "I (insert your full name) hereby finish and close my ritual work. May my magick be heard by the universe and help me obtain my desires. I thank my spiritual guides and higher self for being present today and lending me their hands during this spell work."

Feel free to alter the invocations to fit your own needs.

The Power of Written Word

Words rule the way we express ourselves, and writing is an act of creation. Our desires are more likely to manifest when we take the time to write them out, which is why I suggest writing a spiritual petition every time you do a spell. It is also incredibly important that you write things down in the past tense, as if they have already happened. An effective petition would look something like the following:

"Today, I declare that through my will and powerful spell work, I easily attract and have an abundance of suitors who are interested in dating me." (You can replace the end of that sentence with any specific outcome you want to achieve.)

The Power of Speaking Things into Existence

Even though you have put the spell in writing, it is equally important to speak it into existence. Once your petition has been written, using a commanding voice, read it out loud at your altar. Give yourself a moment to feel the vibrations of your words. Continue to read this petition aloud once a day until the results of the spell manifest.

The Importance of Inner Work in the Mind

Magick is how you influence your reality, both in your inner and outer world. In magick, we have two "temples" in which to perform spiritual work that correspond with these worlds.

Our mind is the first and most powerful temple. It is a gateway for how we imagine our craziest desires. In many ways, the mind is our spiritual playground, where we experiment and make change. The mind doesn't constrain us and it is here that we can perform powerful alchemy to change our reality. To successfully perform magick, we must ensure that our mind-body connection is healthy and balanced. Analyze your relationship with yourself and build a strong practice of self-love before you get started with love magick. We must make sure that we embody the energetic frequencies of love toward ourselves before we try to love anybody else. Once you hone in on this power, you will see that some of the most powerful magick actually happens when you change your own energy. Try your best to be optimistic and have a growth mind-set. With internal spiritual work, it is possible to become exactly who you want to be.

The Importance of Outer Work

Performing a ritual with spell work is a powerful way of using your spiritual energy in the conscious world to create an outcome. The second spiritual temple is the one you create in your reality with your sacred space and altar.

You can easily create a ritual space by making the energy of a normal room more conductive to spell work and your intentions. The energy in this space should feel very different from what you feel in other parts of your house. Some rituals ask you to create a sacred space in a specific room, like your bedroom, bathroom, or kitchen. For example, when it comes to sex and seduction magick, give your bed a makeover with fresh sheets and lit candles. Changes in lighting, color, and music can evoke a spiritual mood.

Additionally, it is important to have an altar, or a more permanent sacred space for your spell work. An altar can be any size, but it should be in a private and quiet space. Your altar will be the place where you meditate and burn candles for ritual magick and keep sacred objects like crystals, statues, photos, and flowers to attract positive energies. The altar is typically covered in a colorful cloth, and when it comes to love magick, it's important to work specifically with red, pink, and white. In magick, colors embody certain energies and you can use them to correspond to your needs. Red is associated with love and good luck, while pink has a soft and feminine quality that embodies a loving and supportive energy. If you can't find a red or pink cloth, white is a great substitute because it is the universal color in magick. A white cloth can bring in peace and help you be mindful during rituals.

Magick is most powerful when you feel inspired and have fun, so get creative with your altar setup by working with your intuition and senses to create the best sacred space for you!

Commitment and Repetition

Patience is key in the journey of becoming a witch. Not every spell is going to work, and some rituals will need to be strengthened and repeated. It is important to try again if you fail and to allow the universe to grant you what you want with divine timing. Never question your magick. Simply move on, make adjustments, and try again.

THE ALTAR AND WITCH'S TOOLS

Every witch needs some basic tools to create magick. The potions in this book require this list of witchcraft supplies. Don't feel forced to acquire expensive tools or equipment. The majority of these tools can be found in occult stores or online for decent prices.

Tools You Will Need

- Mortar and pestle

- Assorted herbs

- Carrier oils (sweet almond, avocado, apricot, and grape seed oils and organic essential oils)

- Slow cooker

- Electric coffee or spice grinder (optional)

- A small cauldron, a firesafe dish, or loose-incense holder

- Stainless steel bowls

- Colored candles in red, white, black, and pink

- Crystals and gems such as rose quartz and crystal quartz (for some potions in this book you will have to acquire more crystals)

- Candleholders

- Self-igniting charcoals

- Glass mason jars

- Assorted metal tins

- Assorted bottles with spray tops

- Assorted glass bottles with roll-on tops and droppers

- Measuring cups and spoons

- Pictures of your crushes and intended targets

- Funnel or cheese cloth

- A magick wand (optional)

- Journal or notebook for recording results

- A tarot deck (I suggest every beginner use the Rider-Waite-Smith, which is widely available)

TAROT IN MAGICK

While this book will not dive deep into tarot practice, using cards to receive messages from spirits and develop an intuitive practice, is going to help you in the process of healing. In magick, pictures are very powerful and the tarot is believed to possess a lot of spiritual power because of this. Using images can penetrate the depths of your subconscious and inspire you to obtain their greatness through the use of symbolism on an internal level.

HERBAL MAGICK

Witches believe that plants and herbs possess spiritual properties, and this is why I will be referring to herbs as "spirits." All plants are capable of hearing and holding prayers and intentions, so they are powerful allies in manifestation. Spending time getting to know your ingredients and empowering them is an essential part of magick. To empower an herb, hold it in your hands, voice your appreciation for the herb, and ask it to help you. Herbs will work harder for you as you build a relationship with them over time. One of my favorite techniques for working with plant spirits was taught to me in a vision by an indigenous elder and famous medicinal mushroom healer named María Sabina. Whenever I use this easy technique I find the plant spirit speaks more to me and I can call upon it when I need extra help in healing. To perform this technique all you need is to get a bit creative with your imagination. Visualize what this plant spirit would look like as a human. You can then animate this spirit, and call upon its forces to be around you even when you're not using it. For example, in my visualization for the lavender plant spirit, I think of her as a young girl; she has dark brown skin and is short and dressed in indigenous attire. She is relaxed and curious because she is still a kid. I find this energy brings me a lot of calmness. Have fun with your visualizations and make sure you are using your intuition and writing things down to help with your magick.

Remember to obtain and use skin-safe organic herbs and essential oils from reliable sources.

CANDLE MAGICK

Candles are essential to witchcraft and the practice of brujeria. The candle uses the element of fire which sparks up your manifestations so they may be heard by the universe. Candles come in many colors and shapes, so it is important to choose the right kind of candle for your specific intent. For most love and sex spell work, I suggest using red and pink figure candles in the shapes of couples, penises, vaginas, and hearts. If you can't find colored candles, a white candle is universal and can stand in for any other color. One of the most commonly used (and easily found) candles in brujeria is the seven-day petition glass candle and it can be used as indicated in the spells I've provided you. These candles usually have an etched picture on them relating to your desired outcome. For love and sex spells choose one with hearts, couples, or a hummingbird.

In brujeria and witchcraft, candle magick is done through a process called dressing and carving. Don't let this fancy term frighten you! Candle dressing is pretty easy. Decide what kind of candle you want for your spell. Then, use a carving knife or sharp tool to write the name of your intended target and a short petition on the candle (this works for taper candles and shape candles only). Place your candle on a tray or plate and generously coat the magickal oil of your choice on your candle. Then, use the herbal powder or crushed herbs for your spell and add to the body of the candle to increase the magick. In this book, I will provide you with guidance on the types of herbs you will be using in each candle spell. After you choose or make a magical powder or herbal candle mixture, roll your candle in the corresponding crushed dried herbs or sprinkle them on top until there is a generous coating. Once the candle is carved with a petition and covered in these ingredients, you can bring it to your altar and begin your spell. In advanced witchcraft practice, you can take some time to interpret any significant candle shapes in the wax. On the altar, let the candle burn completely down and analyze any significant shapes using your intuition.

The second way to dress a candle is to use crushed herbs and oils using seven-day glass candles. Commonly sold in botanicas, they come in many different colors and carry images of various saints, angels and deities. Choose the glass candle that best suits your needs. Poke four to five holes in the wax and use your dropper to dress the candle with oil (eight to ten drops of spell oil should be plenty). Then, crush and empower your selected herbs, sprinkle them on your candle, and burn the candle during your ritual. Since you can't carve a seven-day glass candle, it is important to write down a petition or prayer so that you incorporate writing into the ritual. After you've written an efficient spell, place (or tape onto the glass) the paper right next to your candle and keep it on your altar until the candle is done burning.

CRYSTAL MAGICK

Crystals and minerals have incredible healing properties. They are often used in magick to enhance spell work and can be infused into magick potions. Crystals are very powerful on their own, but to optimize your magick, it is essential that you cleanse and program them.

There are a few common ways to wipe a crystal of past energy. You can either use an energy-cleansing herb like lavender, rosemary, or frankincense to purify the crystal with smoke or you can place the crystal in a bowl of salt and leave it there overnight. Holding the crystal and visualizing that a white light is cleansing it can also be effective. Once you have cleansed the crystal, it is ready for you to program an intention into it. I suggest holding each crystal close to your heart and whispering your deepest intent to them. Invest the most emotional energy you can to see the best results. For the recipes in this book, I suggest using only polished and tumbled crystals because oil and salt will not destroy them. A tumbled crystal is a shiny, small crystal that has been polished down into a small size and does not have any rough edges and therefore isn't vulnerable to the elements. A polished crystal has a smooth feeling and it will not deteriorate when it is placed in a potion. To be successful in doing the magick in this book, it is important you do thorough research on whether or not your crystal will deteriorate if exposed to liquid or oil.

VIBRATION & SELF-LOVE

All acts of magick must begin within you. One of the most important parts of practicing magick is changing your own vibration, which will help you embody a more divine energetic frequency. Society makes it really hard for many people (especially women) to love themselves, and when it comes to magick, this habit of self-loathing depletes one's own spiritual power.

For many reasons, it is important to consistently build a positive relationship with yourself. Magick and spell work can help if you struggle with confidence or self-love. For example, glamour magick can enhance beauty and confidence both on the inside and outside. I suggest that you perform all the self-love and healing rituals in this book to develop a deep practice of love for yourself before you try to obtain a lover with magick. The more positive energy you can generate from within, the more you will attract others.

MAGICAL POWDERS

Magical powders are another important witch's tool. They are especially useful if you're trying to be discreet with your magick. Powders can be made two ways. If you are a fan of the old-fashioned method, use a mortar and pestle to grind your herbs to a powder-like consistency. The second method, using a coffee grinder, saves you time and results in a much finer powder. Herbal powders can be used in scented sachets, in house magick, and for candle dressing.

BATH POTIONS

Want to hear some excellent news? Baths are an important part of doing magick. If you take one before you perform a ritual, it can cleanse you, protect you, and magnify the energy of your intent. Make sure to create a ritual environment for your bath by lighting candles and dropping a rose quartz crystal into your tub.

To make a quick spiritual bath, use a clean bowl to mix your dry ingredients and herbs. I prefer to use Epsom salt and baking soda as bases for baths because they contain detoxifying and healing properties (another plus is that they can help soothe your muscles).

I recommend repeating bath magick at least twice a week for an entire month, or until you see its maximum effect.

CHAPTER 2

OILS FOR SPELL WORK

MAKING MAGICKAL OILS

Oil-making is an essential tool in brujeria as well as in other magick practices. It is an ancient way to strengthen manifestation and anoint oneself for sacred practices. The making of magickal oils is a two-step process. First, you have to make the mother batch of oil by choosing one of the two oil-making methods described below to infuse your herbs. Then, you add the essential oils to customize its scent. The secret to great oil-making is using your sense of smell to craft the perfect potion.

THE ALTAR-INFUSION METHOD

The first oil-making method requires the most amount of time, but it is easier to prepare. Start by gathering the dried herbs in the recipe and placing them all in a clean quart-sized glass jar. Top the herbs with your mix of carrier oil. Seal the jar tightly. Place it on the altar, leaving it there for three to four weeks. Shake the jar every day to spread the ingredients evenly.

After three to four weeks, strain the herbs out of the oil with a funnel or cheesecloth. Fish out any large leftover roots and pour the mother oil into smaller bottles with dropper tops if you desire. It is totally fine if some residue is left in the oil. In fact, the perfect spell oil contains small bits of plant material and larger roots from the infusion.

THE SLOW COOKER METHOD

For the second you can use a heat-based method, for which you will need to use your slow cooker. Add your charmed herbs to the slow cooker and top them with the indicated carrier oil. Set the temperature from 100 to 120 degrees Fahrenheit. I recommend using the lowest heat setting or the "warm setting" to prevent scorching. It is helpful to use a thermometer to monitor the temperature of the oil. You should let the herbs heat up for eight to twelve hours. Check the oil every couple of hours to prevent it from burning, especially towards the end.

Once the oil has cooled, strain the raw plant material using a cheesecloth or funnel. Pour your mother batch oil into small glass bottles with droppers, ensuring that some raw plant material is transferred to each bottle or into a large mason jar. If a recipe contains a large, powerful root that shouldn't be discarded, remove it from the infusion and finely chop it to move it back into the small dropper bottles or large quart-sized mason jar.

Add any additional essential oils that are required by your recipe, then give the bottle a shake to even out the mixture. The magick oil is ready for use once it has cooled and can be used to ritually anoint yourself and your personal objects, to dress candles for spell work, and to increase the potency of bath potions. Also, some oil infusions can be used to create salves and so much more.

F*CKBOY PROTECTION OIL

SUGGESTED TAROT CARD: Strength (VIII)

The dating world can be hard, especially with cheating and dishonesty. The emergence of the term *f*ckboy*, which describes the type of man who manipulates and uses partners, proves this to be true. Fortunately, magick can help dispel this type of energy and person from your life.

Use this oil to perform a spell on yourself that protects you when it comes to encountering bad relationships or sexual encounters. NOTE: This oil is NOT safe for use on skin and is designed for use in spell work only.

YOU WILL NEED
1 large devil's shoestring root • ¼ cup dried rue • 3½ cups sweet almond oil, coconut oil, or olive oil • ¼ cup dried mullein • ¼ cup dried hyssop • 10 strong coffee beans • 12 drops lemongrass essential oil • 1 large glass jar • Small glass bottles with a dropper top (optional)

TIMING
Full Moon

METHOD

Prepare this oil using the slow cooker method or altar-infusion method described on page 24. Once you have made the infused herbal oil, pour the oil into a large mason jar. This will form what we call the "mother batch" of oil which you can store and then pour into smaller dropper bottles as necessary.

Remove the devil's shoestring root from the mother batch and cut it into small pieces, then add a bit of the chopped devil's shoestring root into each of the small dropper bottles. If you're keeping your oil in the large mason jar instead of opting for small bottles, add your essential oil mixture, drop by drop, until it reaches your desired scent. Seal the bottles or jar and let them sit on the altar for one full night. The oil will then be ready to use in your spell work.

RITUAL SUGGESTION

Use this spell oil to dress a penis, vagina, or gender-neutral shaped candle, carved with your petition and full name. Burn the candle and save the protective remnants to keep on your altar or in a charm bag. Repeat this spell monthly, on the Full Moon, to protect yourself against negative energy. For the incantation say, *Today I conjure up the spirit of my protectors. I command these spirits to come into my potion and change my character. Weak I will be no more. My spiritual energy is protected for sure. Eagle, Snake, Mexican spirits of love and war, my wounded heart has suffered enough, can't take anymore. I call upon you to protect my soul. Nobody can hurt me now, I have full control.*

POST-BREAKUP BANISHING OIL

SUGGESTED TAROT CARD: The Justice Card (XI)

This spell oil is crafted with herbs that help with the banishment of a person from your life after a bad breakup. Banishment magick is useful to keep exes at a distance or completely out of your life. It is also a very powerful way to help yourself let go of energy attached to your old partners. NOTE: This oil is NOT safe for use on skin and is designed for use in spell work only.

YOU WILL NEED

½ tablespoon sulfur powder • 1½ cups castor oil • ⅓ cup dried basil • ⅓ cup dried rosemary • 1 teaspoon red chili powder • 1 large mason jar (or small glass bottles with a dropper top) • Funnel or cheesecloth

TIMING

Waning Moon or Dark Moon

METHOD

Prepare this oil using the altar-infusion method described on page 24. (This should not be prepared in your slow cooker because it contains sulfur.) Once the indicated time has passed, and you have made the infused herbal oil from your dried and empowered herbs, pour the oil into a clean large mason jar using a funnel or cheese-cloth. This oil will form what we call the "mother batch" of oil, which you can store and use until you run out. You can also pour the oil into smaller dropper bottles. Seal the bottles or jar and let them sit on the altar for one full night. The oil will then be ready to use in spell work.

RITUAL SUGGESTION

Once the oil is sealed in the glass dropper bottle, let it sit on your altar for three days and whisper the provided incantation to the bottle every night. Anoint a black taper candle with the banishing oil and go outside to cast your spell. Circle your house while holding the candle and envision drawing a white protective circle around the home. Place the candle on your altar, let it burn all the way down, and bury the protective wax remnants of your spell in front of your home. For the incantation say, *Justice, Justice I summon you today. Spirits who embody fairness, to you I pray. I have faith that by my word and will, my bound-aries are drawn. So may be the spirit of _____ forever be gone. And so this magick in me makes a change. I am surrounded by light and nothing is strange. Spirit of justice, oh enter this potion. Bubble bubble, toil and trouble, my heart is at rest, goodbye to commotion.*

SCENTED HAIR AND NAIL OIL

SUGGESTED TAROT CARD: The Empress or Emperor

This exquisite oil is simple to make, and is a perfect gift for your partner to show them that you care. This oil is made with herbs that will strengthen hair and skin, and keep them nice and soft. Trust me, you won't be able to keep your hands off them! The scent of tangerine is refreshing, and will help both partners feel uplifted. It can also be greatly used as a beard or cuticle oil. All of these herbs and oils are skin safe.

YOU WILL NEED

1 cup argan oil • ¼ cup pomegranate seed oil • 1 mason jar • 10–15 drops cedar wood essential oil • 10–20 drops tangerine essential oil • 1 small bottle with a dropper top

TIMING

Any Moon phase

METHOD

Combine the argan and pomegranate seed oils in a mason jar to create a carrier mix. Follow by adding your essential oil drops, one by one, until you achieve a woodsy and refreshing scent. This oil potion does not need to be exposed to heat. Once you have achieved your desired scent, transfer part of the mother batch into a small bottle with a dropper.

RITUAL SUGGESTION

Wrap a bottle of freshly made hair and nail oil in red tissue paper and gift it to your boo on a special occasion. Instruct them to apply six to eight drops to beard and chest, or to hair daily after they cleanse. This oil is incredibly beneficial for the cuticles to help healthy nail growth. For the incantation say, *My lover, my lover, I so gift this to thee. Sensual and Juicy pomegranate please give ___ (lover's name) your divine energy. I pray to the spirits of healing and love. To infuse their magick from the heavens above. The Emperor the Empress full of power, Elevate my lover and let them flower. Connect my lover to inner and outer beauty. Now they always believe that they are a cutie. When I seal this potion my work here is done. Please remind my partner that I love them a ton.*

SACRED SEX COUPLE'S ANOINTING OIL

SUGGESTED TAROT CARDS:
The Lovers & The King of Wands

This oil is designed to use in ritual with a partner to encourage connection and passion in your sex life.

YOU WILL NEED

2 polished lapis lazuli crystals • 3 small polished amethyst crystals • ¼ cup dried skullcap • ¼ cup dried leaves calea zacatechichi • ¼ cup dried blue lotus petals • 2 quart-sized glass jars • 3½ cups sweet almond oil, as a carrier • 4 frankincense pearls • 4–10 drops lemongrass essential oil • 4–10 drops frankincense essential oil • 4–6 drops lavender essential oil • Small glass bottles with a dropper top (optional)

TIMING

Full Moon

METHOD

Using the altar-infusion method (page 24), place your crystals and blessed dried herbs into a quart-sized glass jar and then pour the carrier oil on top of them.

Allow the mixture to infuse for three to four weeks, then,

using a funnel, pour the mother batch into a new quart-sized jar. Add the essential oils to reach the desired scent. If desired, after infusing for the indicated time, pour some of the mother batch of your oil mixture into smaller dropper bottles. Leave the top third of the bottle open to add a few petals of dried blue lotus, the frankincense pearls, and the essential oils to your small dropper bottle. Fill the rest of the bottle with the mother batch oil and shake it to distribute herbs evenly. Keep the mother batch for future uses.

RITUAL SUGGESTION

Right before sex, anoint your third eye by dabbing the oil in between your eyebrows. If doing this with a partner, ask them to close their eyes while you anoint the area for them, then, allow them to reciprocate the gesture. You and your partner can also anoint other erogenous zones of the body like the neck, breasts, and in between the legs. It is useful to anoint the inner legs closer to the knees to prevent any oil from getting into the genitals. For the incantation say, *Caliente—(call-ee-en-teh) Caliente. So bonded are we. And so together, we wish upon this potion times three (anoint yourself and then repeat this incantation three times). Open our eyes, spirit, let us dive deep. So may our sex leave us swept off our feet. Today and always, we make magick in bed. Let us bond on this day, and see the bright future ahead.*

COUPLES BAY-LEAF WISHING OIL

SUGGESTED TAROT CARD: Ace of Pentacles

Spell work can be more powerful if two or more people are performing the energetic work together. Create this potion if you and your partner want to manifest something in tandem. I recommend doing this spell when you are working on a huge couples goal, like buying a new home, or planning a wedding or pregnancy.

YOU WILL NEED

3½ cups sweet almond oil • 13 bay leaves • ¼ cup of mugwort • 4–5 star anise pods • 10–20 drops orange or tangerine essential oil • 1 large glass jar

TIMING

Any Moon cycle

METHOD

For this particular oil, think of thirteen powerful wishes you want to make with your partner. Whisper the wishes to the bay leaf in the affirmative and bless them, then place them in your mother batch oil for heating.

Once you have made the infused herbal oil from your dried and empowered herbs using the slow cooker or altar-infusion method, add your essential oil mixture drop by drop. Seal the mother batch jar and shake it to distribute the herbs and oils evenly. This oil is immediately ready for use in spell work.

RITUAL SUGGESTION

Use this oil to dress a green candle you have carved with your desires. With your partner, write your wishes for manifestation on thirteen bay leaves, and take turns burning them with the candle. Spend five to ten minutes together meditating in front of the altar. Speak your wishes aloud and seal the deal with a kiss or sex session. You can also use this oil to create a couples vision board by anointing it lightly with oil before you hang it in a prominent place. For the incantation say, *Thirteen wishes today have been spoken. Divine universe we thank you, receive this sacred oil as our token. Our power is now multiplied by two so shall our craziest manifestations come true. Universe, universe, we ask that you hear our prayers. Thank you for always giving us our fair share we promise to work hard to reach our goals. One, two, three and now we are whole.*

PEACEFUL RELATIONSHIP OIL

SUGGESTED TAROT CARD: Queen of Cups

This potion really taps into the power of holy basil, which I consider to be a "doctor" of herbs. This plant spirit is calming, uplifting, and healing and can help you solve tension and problems, as well as help you petition to get a lover back.

YOU WILL NEED

6–10 drops basil essential oil • 10 drops lemon essential oil • 3½ cups sweet almond oil • ¼ cup dried holy basil • ¼ cup dried chamomile flowers • ¼ cup dried jasmine buds • ¼ cup dried pink rosebuds • 1 large glass jar

TIMING

Seven days before the Full Moon

METHOD

Once you have made the infused herbal oil from your dried and empowered herbs using the slow cooker or altar-infusion method and the indicated time has passed, add your essential oil mixture drop by drop to the mother batch. Seal the mother batch jar and shake it to distribute the herbs and oils evenly. This oil is immediately ready for use in spell work.

Use this oil to heal after fights and to ease conflict when it occurs in your home. Rub a bit of oil on a handwritten apology letter and give to your beloved. You can also dress a couples candle or a green seven-knob candle carved with your and your partner's names to bring them back after a separation and pray for seven days that they come back to you. For the incantation say, *This oil contains some master healers. I summon their spirits because I am a dreamer. Sacred basil, chamomile, jasmine, and rose. Divine flowers, that today I have chose. Bring resolution, eliminate pain. Work your magick, and all arguments tame. So may my beloved come back to me, with their free will so mote it be.*

THE HONEY JAR POTION

Honey is often used in magick to attract things. This honey jar spell is designed to bring a crush closer to you or increase the possibility of someone falling in love with you.

YOU WILL NEED

1 small clear glass jar with a lid •
½–1 cup honey • 1 tablespoon dried damiana •
1 tablespoon dried roses • mortar and pestle •
2–3 cinnamon sticks

TIMING

Seven days leading up to the Full Moon

METHOD

Pour your honey into the jar until the jar is three-quarters of the way full. Crush and empower your damiana and roses in a mortar and pestle to a fine consistency, then add them into the honey. Add the whole cinnamon sticks. Swirl the herbs around the honey until they are well-incorporated.

After you have prepared your honey and placed it on top of your altar, take a small piece of paper and write the following petition on the paper then say, *I cast a spell upon this altar with the Two of Cups please give my intended lover a friendly bump. Bring them closer to me, not out of force, allow them to come of their own accord. Fuse our energies, and bond us at the core. True love will form in due time for sure. My dream relationship is now reality, by my spellwork and faith, I allow the universe to give me the key. Open the heart of my intended lover. I deserve this, and now all is covered.*

Put a picture of your intended target on top of the jar. Seal the jar and pray upon it daily in the seven days leading up to the Full Moon. On the Full Moon, burn a small pink, red, or white candle dressed with love attracting oil (page 45) to finalize the spell. Wait for one month to see if the spell manifests and, if necessary, repeat it until your petition comes true.

You can also coat an apple carved with your crush's name with the honey and eat it with gusto, focusing on your love intention on the same day.

12 FULL MOON SOULMATE ATTRACTING CANDLE

SUGGESTED TAROT CARD: The Moon

Magick can sometimes be more effective if it's carried out over a longer period of time. For this massive manifestation, you can work with the energy of the Moon (which rules over our emotions) to manifest a possible soulmate. Therefore, it is incredibly important to incorporate the Moon into rituals for love. This candle works with silver and blue, and is loaded with Full Moon herbs and crystals to supercharge your soul's desire.

YOU WILL NEED

1 (12–14 oz.) glass jar with wick attached •
3 tumbled moonstones • 12 jasmine buds •
½ tablespoon of chamomile flowers • 1 star
anise pod • ½ teaspoon of poppy seeds •
Mortar and pestle • Microwave-safe bowl •
1 bag of microwaveable soy wax • 25–35 drops
clary sage essential oil • Blue candle dye •
2 pinches silver glitter

TIMING

Pour two to three days before a Full Moon

Candle-making is all about taking your sweet time to create something beautiful and filled with intention. Meditate on true love and your soul's desire while you create this hand-poured candle.

Start by preparing your jar for the candle-pouring process by attaching the cotton wick to the bottom of your jar with a glue gun (you can skip this step if you bought a jar with the wick attached). Put your three crystals at the bottom of the jar. (The three crystals represent you, your soulmate, and your spiritual guides and the Moon.)

Then crush the jasmine, chamomile, one star anise pod, and poppy seeds (all herbs of the Moon) into a fine powder with your mortar and pestle or spice grinder. Set the powder aside for dressing.

Next, in a microwave-safe bowl melt two cups of soy wax on high for 3 minutes (be sure that you do not burn the wax or cause an explosion). If you need additional time for the wax to liquify, go in 30-second increments.

The candle pouring happens in steps so you can have layers of herbs and scents. Add drops of the clary sage essential oil and dye into your wax until you reach your desired smell and color (a light blue will truly embody the energy of the Moon). Slowly pour your first layer of wax until you fill about one third of the jar. Let the wax cool for about 30–40 minutes then add the crushed herb mix to the top. Repeat the steps two more times until the jar is full. Leave the candle on your altar to cool overnight. Once it is completely solid, top your candle with love manifesting oil, crushed jasmine, and silver glitter.

RITUAL SUGGESTION

Start by burning the candle on the Full Moon. Write down the petition below, then read it aloud. Let your candle burn for fifteen minutes, and then snuff it out (never blow a candle out during the ritual). Let it sit until the next Full Moon. For the incantation say, *The Moon is a miracle worker who connects us to love. Divine Mistress of the Moon, you shine light from above. I petition you tonight to ask that you help. For twelve Full Moon nights, my deepest desires will be heard and felt. I intend to manifest the partner of my dreams. I honor you many nights, and we make a great team. Please grant me my soul mate within less than a year. I am open to love, and have faith in you, so I lose all my fear.*

LOVE ATTRACTING OIL

SUGGESTED TAROT CARD: The Fool (Card 0)

This is a general love magick oil that you can use in spell work to increase your chances of finding love or a soul mate, or to capture someone you've had your eyes on.

YOU WILL NEED

3½ cups sweet almond oil • 15–20 drops vanilla essential oil • ¼ cup of dried hibiscus • ¼ cup dried damiana • 1 finely chopped vanilla bean • 3 cinnamon sticks • 2 star anise pods • 1 large glass jar • Small glass bottles with a dropper top (optional)

TIMING

A week after the New Moon (when the Moon is most powerful for new beginnings)

METHOD

Once you have made the infused herbal oil from your dried and empowered herbs using the slow cooker or altar-infusion method, add your essential oil mixture drop by drop to the mother batch. Seal the mother batch jar and shake it to distribute the herbs and oils evenly. This oil is immediately ready for use in spell work. If you desire, pour some of the mother batch of oil into smaller dropper bottles for portable and easier use. If you choose to use smaller bottles, remove the vanilla bean from the mother mixture, chop it, and add four to five pieces into each small bottle.

RITUAL SUGGESTION

Dress a heart-shaped or seven-day love candle with this oil and write a petition to attract your desired lover. Burn the candle on your love altar next to a picture of your desired boo and place the petition next to the candle. For the incantation say, *The Fool is adventurous, silly and bold. May I embody his energy and manifest a lover that's gold. I have faith in my magick, so these candles I dress. Finding love is now easy, and I lose all my stress. I desire this lover with divine timing. To the top, to the top, on the mountain of love I am climbing. I believe in my power to make this happen. This lover is mine, and just like Cupid, their heart I'm kidnapping.*

LUST OIL

This is an oil you can use to manifest better sex or just sex in general. This oil is not coercive and it works by increasing the chances you will run into someone who is sexually interested in you. Wear it when you go out, especially, on your chest and breasts, the area of the belly right above your pelvis, or behind your ears and on your neck. You can also anoint a necklace with this oil or fill a small vial to hang on a necklace if you prefer not to wear it on your body. As an added benefit, the jezebel root is believed to help people attract wealthy partners.

YOU WILL NEED

3½ cups sweet almond oil • 2–3 ginseng roots • ⅛ cup jezebel root • ¼ cup dried patchouli leaves • ¼ cup dried damiana • 12–15 drops patchouli essential oil • 1 large glass jar • Small glass bottles with a dropper top (optional)

TIMING

Make this oil on the Full Moon (the Full Moon can help supercharge your oil and is said to be sensual in nature)

METHOD

Once you have made the infused herbal oil from your dried and empowered herbs using the slow cooker or altar-infusion method, add your essential oil mixture drop by drop to the mother batch. Seal the mother batch jar and shake it to distribute the herbs and oils evenly. This oil is immediately ready for use in spell work. If you desire, pour some of the mother batch of oil into smaller dropper bottles for portable and easier use. If you choose to use smaller bottles, remove all of the roots used, chop them finely, and add four to five pieces into each small bottle.

RITUAL SUGGESTION

Dress a penis- or vagina-shaped candle with this oil and burn it to attract sex and passion into your life. Let the candle burn while you masturbate and come to an orgasm. Have fun fantasizing about your ideal partner as you reach climax. Snuff out the candle every time after you masturbate and repeat the ritual as often as you want to attract sex. For the incantation say, *On my command, The Knight of Wands comes swooping in. And I call in sexual pleasure with a huge grin. Out there is someone who I can attract. Divine sexual connection comes in a snap. I am confident and magnetic, people are attracted to me. And so may I have all the sex I want, consensually.*

MEXICAN ROAD-OPENING OIL
FOR LOVE

SUGGESTED TAROT CARD: The Chariot

The *abre camino* or road-opening spell is common in brujeria and is designed to remove spiritual blockages to love. This spell is especially useful if you have been single for a while and want to change that.

For this spell you will also need to collect dirt at night, when no one can see you, from a crossroad (where two streets meet). Bring an offering of herbs, liquor, or candy and petition the spirits that live there to open the roads of love for you. Gather the dirt and bring it back to use in your candle work.

YOU WILL NEED

1 cup abre camino herb • 3½ cups sweet almond oil • ¼ cup catnip • 6 juniper berries • 7–10 drops rose otto essential oil • 2–5 drops jasmine essential oil • ¼ cup pink rosebuds • 1 large glass jar • Small glass bottles with a dropper top (optional) • 1 vanilla bean

TIMING

On a Wednesday (ruled by Mercury, who opens roads), or a Thursday (ruled by Jupiter, the planet of luck and abundance)

Once you have made the infused herbal oil from your dried and empowered herbs using the slow cooker or altar-infusion method, add your essential oil mixture drop by drop to the mother batch. Seal the mother batch jar and shake it to distribute the herbs and oils evenly. This oil is immediately ready for use in spell work. If you desire, pour some of the mother batch of oil into smaller dropper bottles for portable and easier use. If you choose to use smaller bottles, remove the vanilla bean, chop it, and add four to five pieces into each small bottle.

Use this oil to dress a seven-day road-opening glass candle or a key shaped candle and burn at your altar. You should grind some abre camino herb in your mortar and pestle and combine it with your crossorads dirt to dress the candle. Images of keys or an antique key on your altar can help increase the success of this spell. Often road opening candles come in two colors (green and orange) the color of this candle doesn't matter as much for this working as the fact that it says road opening. For the incantation say, *I have the power to open the roads that have previously been blocked in my life. I am tired of not finding love, my life needs some spice. Abre camino, whose spirit I use today. Remove all obstacles out of my way. I remove all mental, physical, and spiritual blockages. Out of my way bad luck and any other damages. Abran mi camino brujas divinas. (Aw-bran mee ca-mee-no broo-has dee-vee-nas). Work your miracle magick for me, so that I can be fulfilled and this work be finished.*

VENUS PLANETARY OIL

SUGGESTED TAROT CARD: Four of Wands

The planet Venus is said to strengthen all spell work related to love. In Roman mythology, the goddess of love and sex was named Venus, so you can petition her with this oil if this fits your personal practice. Use this oil in all candle spells and bath recipes to amplify your efforts and to attract Venus energy, which will assist you in your efforts. This oil contains grapeseed oil as a carrier base because grapes are considered a favorite of the Goddess Venus.

YOU WILL NEED

2 cups apricot seed oil • 1½ cups grapeseed oil • 4–6 balm of Gilead buds • ¼ cup dried yarrow flowers • ⅛ cup dried jasmine buds • 10–15 drops rose otto essential oil • 1 large glass jar • Small glass bottles with a dropper top (optional)

TIMING

On a Friday, which is considered Venus's day

METHOD

Once you have made the infused herbal oil from your dried and empowered herbs using the slow cooker or altar-infusion method, add your essential oil mixture drop by drop to the mother batch. Seal the mother batch jar and shake it to distribute the herbs and oils evenly. This oil is immediately ready for use in spell work. If you desire, pour some of the mother batch of oil into smaller dropper bottles, remove some of the buds and flowers from the mother mixture, and add four to five pieces into each small bottle.

RITUAL SUGGESTION

Carve the planetary symbol of Venus onto two red or pink taper candles. Anoint them with the oil and burn them on your altar to draw in the power of Venus while performing love and sex spell work. These can be used with any other rituals described in this book to amplify it's power. The oil can also be used to light the candles before sex magick. Lastly, add this oil to your love baths to increase their potency. For the incantation say, *Queen of the planets, who embodies love, sex and grace. I summon your power from outer space. Amplify my beauty and save me from pain. Oh revered planet of Venus, I don't come in vain. I take my spellwork seriously, and speak from the heart. Please let love come to me like a work of art. Venus o Venus, you always pull through. Thank you for working for me, and being so true.*

CHAPTER 3

ATTRACTION AND LOVE MANIFESTING

THE ETHICS OF LOVE AND SEX MAGICK

Many people believe that doing love and sex magick is unethical. While this is a valid concern, there are many ways to practice love magick that are based in consent. You can incorporate words into your magick that will allow your intended target to maintain their free will. When you perform a written spell petition, insert a line that specifically mentions free will and consent of the individual you are targeting. Here's an example of how to write a love spell to attract a partner without force.

(Insert person's name) has a crush on me, and their love will grow for me through this spell, ONLY if it is through their natural desire and will. May love never be forced out of this person unless it comes from their heart.

Before proceeding with any spell work, check with your gut feeling. Is this something that you would be okay with if it was done to you? If the answer is yes and you don't foresee any regrets, proceed wholeheartedly. I can attest that the spell work in this book is not dark magick. It is designed to heighten your own vibration and help you on your journey to living a happy and fulfilling life.

I believe that love magick is a form of flattery and a great way to start a relationship with someone. When someone puts love behind a spell intended to capture your heart, they are professing their deepest desires toward you. A cute personal story: A lover of mine actually confessed that he had performed a magickal ritual to attract me, and I found it very sweet that he used his magick to bring me closer. We had a beautiful relationship and continue to be friends even after our breakup!

DREAMS OF YOUR LOVER INCENSE

SUGGESTED TAROT CARD: The High Priestess

Dream magick is very popular among witches. Dreams are said to reveal our deepest desires and our subconscious thoughts, so it's important to pay close attention to them!

YOU WILL NEED

¼ cup white copal • ⅛ cup dragon's blood resin • ½ tablespoon mugwort • ½ tablespoon damiana • ½ tablespoon lavender • ½ tablespoon calea zacchatechi • Mortar and pestle or spice grinder • Self-igniting charcoal blocks (needed each time you burn this incense) • A firesafe incense burner or a cauldron • 1 glass container

TIMING

Before bedtime on a Wednesday or Friday

METHOD

Crush all your dried and empowered herbs individually with your mortar and pestle (or spice grinder). Then combine them all to create a powder that you can sprinkle on top of the charcoal blocks. If you have any leftover incense, store it in a glass container and save for another day.

To perform dream magick, all you need is a notebook or journal to observe your dreams when you wake up. Before bed, say a prayer or incantation to program your mind to have vivid and prophetic dreams. Don't fear if you are not an expert at interpreting! Use your intuition or search dream symbolism on the internet (you can find one from Cosmo at https://www.cosmopolitan.com/sex-love/advice/g3112/sex-dreams). In addition, this spell can help you ask general questions about your lover. Burn this incense near your bed before going to sleep and meditate with the smoke for ten minutes. Repeat ritual every other day for a week, and keep track of your dreams with the exact dates that they occur. For the incantation, hold your hands over your incense powder (or wave your magick wand clockwise) and say these words out loud:

As I enter the dream world, I receive accurate messages, pictures, and details about my soul mate and where I will meet them. From this spiritual work many answers will stem. Sacred incense, sacred fire, tonight in the dream world, clarity shall come. Off into a deep sleep now I become. I call upon your wisdom to reveal the answer to my soul's question, (insert the general questions) Spirits of the fire, now all worry is lessened.

LOVE DRAWING ENERGY SPRAY

SUGGESTED TAROT CARD: The Lovers

Every witch needs some easy, on-the-go magick for when full rituals are not an option. This potion is designed to help you attract love and attention from your crushes when you're away from home. Pull the Lovers card out from the tarot deck. When you are done making this spray, place it on top of the card and pray to the spirits contained in that card.

YOU WILL NEED

3 fl. oz. witch hazel • 1 3 oz. glass bottle with spray top • 25–30 drops patchouli essential oil • 6–10 drops blood orange essential oil • 10–12 drops neroli essential oil

TIMING

Friday, the day of love magick

METHOD

Pour the witch hazel into your glass bottle and leave the top third of the bottle open for essential oils. One by one, add each essential oil and blend it until you reach your desired scent. The dominant notes in this potion should be patchouli and blood orange. Feel free to adjust to your liking by adding more or less essential oil drops.

RITUAL SUGGESTION

Place the bottle on your love altar and ask that this spray helps you attract the person you're interested in. After letting the bottle sit for three days, carry it with you whenever you anticipate being around the person you desire. Spray the potion generously on yourself and areas where you will encounter your bae. You can also use this to spray yourself and your altar before you perform ritual work to enhance the love-drawing energy. For the incantation say, *So may love not evade me no more. In this life I choose to be rich in love, not poor. By the power vested in me, I chant this incantation times three. Spirit guides, Goddess, assist me in finding a good love match for my heart so may I be assisted in finding my true love.*

If you have the name of a desired lover, you can ask the spirits of the Lovers card (Adam and Eve) or another love goddess to aid you in obtaining your desired target's attention.

SELF-LOVE MIRROR POTION

SUGGESTED TAROT CARD: The Star

This special potion is brewed like a tea. It is empowered by crystals to help you with affirmation and self-love. The potion uses the power of obsidian, a protective stone used often in Mexican divination rituals and rose quartz which is the stone of unconditional love.

YOU WILL NEED

3 cups spring water • ⅓ cup dried mugwort • ⅓ cup dried wormwood • 3–4 star anise pods • French press • 1 quart-sized mason jar • 3 polished obsidian stones or obsidian arrows • 2 polished rose quartz stones • 1 handheld mirror

TIMING

Full Moon

METHOD

For this potion, boil the spring water and steep the loose herbs in a French press (or mason jar) for about 15–20 minutes, until the mixture has a powerful scent. As it brews, whisper your incantation. Once the concoction has cooled, transfer the tea mixture to a quart-sized mason jar, adding the polished obsidian stones and rose quartz. Seal the jar and leave it to absorb the moonlight. This empowered water can be used immediately after it has been charged by the Moon to enchant magical tools.

RITUAL SUGGESTION

Cleanse a handheld mirror of negative energy by using your obsidian and mugwort tea wipe. This will magnify your affirmations and help you create a positive relationship with yourself. Whisper affirmations of self-love during the day and ask the mirror to protect your energy from the evil eye. The obsidian crystals connect us to the spiritual world, so you can speak your truest desires to the mirror and ask for assistance in manifesting love. For the incantation say, *Mirror, Mirror, in my hand in my divine shadow now I stand. From this day on, I so declare, self-hatred I may not bear. These are three things I love about me (insert three affirmations). Through this incantation I am now healed. May my truest desires be revealed.*

GET RID OF DATING ANXIE-TEA

SUGGESTED TAROT CARD: The Hanged Man

A simple blend of herbs that can help reduce anxiety. It's best used on a frequent basis in combination with meditation and mental health therapy to reduce chronic stress related to dating and sex.

YOU WILL NEED

¼ cup dried skullcap • ½ cup dried lemon balm • ½ tablespoon dried lavender • ⅓ cup dried linden flowers • French press, teapot with mesh strainer, or empty tea bags • Water

TIMING

New Moon

METHOD

Combine all of the dried herbs in a French press, a teapot with mesh strainer, or, for individual portions, empty tea bags. Boil the water and pour it over the dried herbs. The expression "bubble, bubble, toil and trouble" really applies here! Steep the tea for fifteen minutes and serve. You know you have made a great tea if it is very steamy and fragrant. The effects are more noticeable after prolonged use (about a week of sipping this tea daily).

Drink this tea before you go out on a date or head out for a night on the town. Develop a relationship with the herbs in this tea by drinking it once a day for a week and meditating for ten minutes every day after consumption. For the incantation say, *Spirit allies, I call upon you to help me overcome my fears and anxiety. I go within, and find the calmness rooted in me. So may I embody the waters calm. Keep my heart safe through the offering of this lemon balm. By the power of three, I know these magical ingredients will help me.* Repeat this line three times and finish while you wave your hand or wand on your tea: *Go. Go. Go. Go away anxiety.*

FEELING MYSELF BEAUTY ENHANCING BATH

SUGGESTED TAROT CARD:
The King of Wands or the Queen of Wands

This bath is the ultimate tool for glamour magick. It is based in the tradition of bathing in green tea to preserve youthfulness.

YOU WILL NEED

⅓ cup green tea powder • 1 tablespoon French green clay • 4 cups Epsom salt • ¼ cup colloidal oatmeal powder (or ground oatmeal) • 1 cup dried roses • 1 bowl • 8–20 drops ylang-ylang essential oil

TIMING

At the beginning of the month (continuing to bathe at least twice weekly for one entire month for enhanced effect)

METHOD

Place all dry ingredients in a clean bowl and distribute them evenly with your hands. Visualize a pink light surrounding your bath mixture. Add the essential oil drop by drop and blend them all together until you achieve your desired scent.

Fill the bathtub with hot water. Add the ingredients and bathe in the hot water for fifteen to twenty minutes. Repeat this bath ritual twice a week for one month. For the incantation say, *Hot water hot water, I speak to thee. Brew this bath potion for a skin softening tea. Vitality, vitality, is alive in this brew. Bath potion, bath potion my soul and body are new. I am energized, blessed and radiate beauty. Bold and confident, falling in love with myself is my duty. Thank you green plants for refreshing my spirit. I now walk around knowing life gets better by the minute.*

CHAPTER 4

SEXUAL AND APHRODISIAC POTIONS

SEX & ORGASM MAGICK

Embracing your sexual energy is a critical part of developing your spiritual powers. After all, at their core humans are very sexual. I love witchcraft as a practice because, unlike certain religions and oppressive societal constructs in our world, it celebrates the sexual power within us rather than stifling it.

In magick, the orgasm is considered a force of nature that aids manifestation. This sexual process heightens our energy because it boosts our serotonin levels, making us happier human beings. This feeling alone can help us build a healthier relationship with our body.

The proper way to perform orgasm magick is to enjoy yourself as much as possible. Focus on a vision or intent while you explore your body. As you feel an orgasm coming, visualize exactly what you want as clearly as possible and let yourself cum. Spend a few minutes afterward meditating on your intention. If you are trying to attract a partner, envision them as you masturbate to climax. This can be an efficient way of bringing them into your life. I recommend masturbating after every magickal ritual to enhance its potency, but you can also perform orgasm magick with a partner if they can make you "O."

Having regular sex and honoring a bond with your partner by performing sex magick is a very special way to strengthen your connection and practice manifestation. When you're with your partner, advocate for your sexual pleasure. Don't be afraid to guide them in helping you see stars. There is no wrong or right way to have sex. If you want to try something different in the bedroom, like BDSM or role-playing, express your desires in healthy ways. Being honest about what you want will help you have an accepting and sex-positive attitude toward yourself and your partner.

Finally, take care of your sexual health by using protection and getting tested for sexually transmitted infections. Sex is most enjoyable when you aren't anxious about STDs or the risk of pregnancy.

CHOCOLATE BODY PAINT FOR COUPLES SIGIL MAGICK

A sigil is a symbol that you create to represent a larger concept or purpose. In the act of creating a symbol, it is believed that you are bringing those desires from your subconscious mind into existence. Traditionally in sigil magick, your spell work has been heard by the universe once the sigil is erased. Sigil magick is often followed by masturbation or sex magick with a partner. Agree upon a common intention for the sigil with your partner and do your best to visualize it manifesting as you orgasm.

YOU WILL NEED

½ cup honey • ⅓ cup tablespoon organic cacao powder • ½ tablespoon melted coconut oil • 1 small bowl • 1 spoon • 1 soft paintbrush for sigil drawing

TIMING

At any time, but best at night

METHOD

Mix together all ingredients until the paint is sticky but not runny, and not so thick that it can't spread on your body easily.

Obtain consent from your partner to participate in this ritual with you and then get naked. Gather your ingredients and empower them with your intentions. In a small bowl, mix all of the ingredients with a spoon until they are well incorporated and you reach a smooth but not drippy consistency. If the paint is not dark enough, add a bit more of cacao powder.

After making the chocolate paint, absorb each other's beauty and then decide on a joint purpose for the sigils. Create the sigil, and using a soft paintbrush, take turns painting it on each other. When you're done, lick it sensually off your partner's favorite erotic spots. (Don't get this mixture near genitals, it may cause yeast infections.) For the incantation say, *Chocolate, Chocolate Open our hearts. Honey is sweet, and we promise to do our part. This act of sex magick is dedicated to you. This sex is so good that our minds it blew. Help us great spirit, as we please each other. Now in love we are both smothered. See our symbols which we so lovingly created. Help us to gain all that we've awaited. Through this ritual we bond as a couple. And so may our abundance and luck be quintupled.*

ORAL SEX LIP SCRUB

SUGGESTED TAROT CARD: Ace of Wands

The lips are an important part of having great sex. Therefore, they should be pampered by special rituals like pampering yourself with a lip scrub. Use it to make your lips soft, kissable, and enticing for a night of passionate oral sex. If you're intimidated by performing oral sex, this sexy potion will make the process more fun and relaxing. It can give you a great boost of confidence on a night when you want to be sexier.

YOU WILL NEED
¼ cup raw sugar • ½ teaspoon honey •
½ teaspoon coconut oil • 1 small bowl •
1 strawberry • 2–3 drops lavender essential oil

TIMING
Any time of the month, but most potent when you know you are going out or seeing someone special

METHOD
Combine the raw sugar, honey, and coconut oil into a small bowl. Smash your strawberry to a fine paste and squeeze out its juices. Add the juice of the strawberry to

the bowl. Then add two to three drops of essential oil of lavender to help you calm your nerves.

Put both hands over your lip scrub and bless it with the incantation. Use the mixture on your lips to exfoliate them and visualize your craziest oral sex fantasy coming true. For the incantation say, *My soft lips are ready to kiss. They are gateway. They are bliss. Sacred acts I perform with my partner in bed. I go down like a god/goddess, my confidence is ten. Today I make my lover's fantasies come true. And so forth, I am a master of sex for me and my boo.*

APHRODISIAC ORAL SEX LIP BALM

SUGGESTED TAROT CARD: The World

This lip balm is for portable sex magick. It encourages positive sexual energy and makes oral sex more fun with its vibrant citrus scent.

YOU WILL NEED

¼ cup grated beeswax or beeswax pastilles • ¼ cup organic cocoa butter chips • 2 tablespoons coconut oil or apricot seed oil • 1 small metal bowl • Double boiler • 2–3 drops cardamom essential oil • 1–3 drops ginger essential oil • 4–5 drops tangerine essential oil • 1 larger lip balm tin or 2 small ones

TIMING

Do this ritual on a day you have a lot of time because melting beeswax can be time consuming. Perform this ritual at nighttime two or three days before the Full Moon and let it ripen on your altar or catch some moonlight on your windowsill for two days leading up to the Full Moon.

METHOD

Place your chopped beeswax, cocoa butter chips, and oils in a small metal bowl and melt it down to liquid consistency using a double boiler. Stir in the essential oils and immediately pour the mixture into the lip balm tin. Allow your balm to cool completely before you cap the containers. The recipe yields one large tin (or two small ones) of lip balm. Be cautious using the ginger and cardamom essential oils because they are very potent! Start with 1-2 drops and add more if you feel it necessary. The smell of cocoa butter and essential oils will be a treat for your lips and nose!

RITUAL SUGGESTION

Before going down on your partner, say the incantation over the balm and apply it to your lips. The ginger and cardamom create warming and tingling sensations, which will create a good time for both of you! I also suggest gifting this balm to your significant other. For the incantation say, *Sexy, sexy time is near. Let my lips be pleasing to my dear. Great spirits of cardamom, ginger, and tangerine let us keep going all night like a sex dream. Sensual power is in the air. Orgasms, memories, and fun on this night we share.*

MORNING ROMP MACA ELIXIR

SUGGESTED TAROT CARD: The Magician

No more excuses for skipping a morning bone sesh! Putting aside time to have sex is very important to preserve a relationship, and this ritual takes the concept of a morning cup of coffee to a new level. This healthy coffee substitute is made with maca powder, matcha green tea, and honey to relieve stress, lift your energy, and reduce your fatigue. This potion can also possibly help people who have trouble reaching orgasm because maca is said to have aphrodisiac properties. This will yield two generous cups of elixir.

YOU WILL NEED

4 cups unsweetened milk, preferably coconut, cashew, or hempseed • ⅛ cup maca powder (increase your dose to reach your desired flavor if you'd like) • 1 tablespoon green matcha powder (or more to taste) • ⅛ cup honey or sugar (sweeten to taste) • 1 tablespoon of coconut oil • Blender

TIMING

Before you make love in the morning, but after anointing each other with your couple's anointing oil (page 34).

METHOD

Combine all of the ingredients in a blender and mix them together on the lowest setting. Serve this "coffee" either hot or cold, adding more honey to taste.

RITUAL SUGGESTIONS

This potion is magick because it helps establish positive habits for couples by encouraging sexual bonding and mindfulness. Take this drink and anoint each other's third eye together on days when you're both off and have plenty of time to get busy in the morning. You can take this herbal elixir every other day to encourage long-term stress reduction and relaxation. For the incantation say, *During morning time our bodies are free. Magician, Magician, it's time to de-stress my partner and me. Green tea, green tea and sexy honey from the bee as we cum together, help us activate our harmony. One, two, three, many orgasms in bed. Divine elixir help us today to get ahead.*

SEX TOY CLEANER

Sex toys can make solo sex and partnered sex more fun and interactive, but many people forget that it's important to wash toys correctly so they don't spread bacteria to your body. This special sex toy cleaner has antibacterial properties.

YOU WILL NEED

1 empty foaming hand dispenser or bottle with pump • 1 12 oz. bottle spring or filtered water • 2 tablespoons castile soap • 2 teaspoons fractionated coconut oil • 15 drops tea tree oil • 8 drops peppermint essential oil • 8 drops eucalyptus essential oil • 6–10 drops rosemary essential oil

TIMING

Any Moon cycle

METHOD

Fill your empty bottle ¾ of the way with water. Add in the castile soap, coconut oil, and essential oils. Shake the bottle to incorporate all ingredients and then fill the rest with water to the top. If your sex toy cleaner is more watery than soapy, add some more castile soap until it reaches a perfect soapy consistency like that of a light body wash.

RITUAL SUGGESTION

Use sex toy cleaner to wash your toys immediately after play. For the incantation say, *Dear Queen of Swords, I declare my body a temple help me keep it clean. I am sacred and protected, thank you for being on my team. I manifest healthy sex, wild fantasies come true, communication, cleanliness, and happiness for my partners and me too.*

SULTRY SANGRIA

SUGGESTED TAROT CARD: Knight of Cups

Enchanted cocktails can do a lot for the mood if they are consumed consensually. Wine and liquor potions were quite common in the old days and were used to celebrate the gods and goddesses of lust and love.

YOU WILL NEED

1 cup fresh blackberries • 2 small sweet apples, sliced thin • 2 oranges, sliced thin • 1 large container or punch bowl • 1 bottle red wine (best to use a medium-dry red wine) • 3 cups orange juice • splash club soda or ginger ale • 4 cinnamon sticks

TIMING

Any time is great for this ritual (It's 5 o'clock somewhere!)

METHOD

This luscious potion is easy to make. Start by blessing your fruits and rub them lightly over your body, paying special attention to the heart and chest area. And yes, rub them over your pelvic area (clothing on) to empower them with sexual energy while fantasizing about your lover. The fruit will be empowered by your energy, so they will have a stronger effect when your lover drinks the potion.

Wash and slice all the fruits, put them in the large container or punch bowl, and add in the wine. Then add the juice, club soda or ginger ale, and four cinnamon sticks. Stir until the ingredients are well-blended. Leave this potion to rest in your fridge until you are ready to serve it.

RITUAL SUGGESTION

Prepare a romantic dinner and offer your lover some sangria in a fancy glass. Enjoy two to three glasses and see where the rest of the night takes you. For the incantation say, *Vino (vee-no), Vino, with my magical powers I enchant you. Knight of Cups, from the bottom of my heart, I speak my desires so true. May my partner crave my body and sense my desire. All of these fruits and wine, together make fire. And so tonight, touch by touch, we never get tired.*

LOVE AND LUST COCKTAIL

SUGGESTED TAROT CARD: Three of Cups

This cocktail uses the magick of rose and pomegranate (associated with the goddess of love and sex) to awaken the senses. Make this cocktail in honor of them and ask that they bestow your relationship with love and passion. If you're single, ask that they grant you a night of passionate great sex.

YOU WILL NEED

FOR THE ROSE SIMPLE SYRUP IN THIS COCKTAIL

Small saucepan • ½ cup spring water •
½ cup of rose water (it is really important you get food grade, not the kind for cosmetic use) • 2 cups granulated sugar • Jar or bottle with tight-fitting lid

FOR THE COCKTAIL BASE

Champagne flute • 1 bottle champagne • 1 tablespoon pomegranate juice, per flute of champagne • Several pomegranate seeds

TIMING

Anytime

METHOD

To prepare the simple syrup, in a small saucepan combine the water, rose water, and sugar. Stir consistently to dissolve the sugar and simmer on low heat for five minutes. Let the liquid cool and strain into a jar or bottle with a tight-fitting lid. Refrigerate until you are ready to use it.

Grab a flute and pour half a glass of champagne. Add about ½ tablespoon of the simple syrup, adding more to taste, then add in the pomegranate juice. Stir and add more champagne. Based on taste, add more rose syrup or champagne to reach your desired flavor. For extra appeal, throw in a couple of pomegranate seeds in the champagne and whisper your intent to them. The redness of their color will amplify the color magick in the cocktail.

RITUAL SUGGESTION

Make sure to honor the occasion with a toast to make it extra special! Serve this to your partner after you bless the cocktail and offer it to the love goddesses to thank her. Leave it on your altar for one night. For the incantation say, *Goddesses of love I summon thee. As I make this cocktail, tonight you come to me. Take this fruit and liquor as a gift, and so the sensual energies in the room may shift. Tonight your magick will be felt. And so my lover into my arms will melt. Many cups of this drink on this night will be shared. Goddesses thank you for all your love and care.*

MASSAGE BAR

SUGGESTED TAROT CARD: Ace of Wands

Your hands are an important part of performing magick. Massaging can be very therapeutic and erotic, so enjoy making this bar when you have plenty of time.

YOU WILL NEED

¼ cup beeswax pastilles or shredded beeswax •
¼ cup melted cocoa butter • ¼ cup coconut oil •
2 tablespoons sweet almond oil • Double boiler •
10 drops cardamom essential oil • 10 drops ginger
essential oil • 15–20 drops patchouli essential
oil • 15–20 coffee beans • Silicone molds or a
muffin tin • 2 tablespoons dried calendula •
2 tablespoons of dried arnica

TIMING

Anytime, but plan accordingly so there is time
to cool down before use

METHOD

Melt the beeswax, cocoa butter, coconut oil, and sweet almond oil in a double boiler over low heat. Be sure to stir the mixture so you do not scorch any of the ingredients. (Your aim is to have a solid bar, with a lot of beeswax, so it is easy to use on your partner. Making this bar is about trial and error, so experiment with what consistency you prefer.) Remove the mixture from the heat and add essential oils as it cools.

Place 10 to 12 coffee beans in the silicone mold for each bar. Lightly crush and add the calendula and arnica (a miraculous skin plant used to help with pain and healing wounds) flowers, placing a few flowers in each mold. Pour in the mixture and let the bars cool for twenty-four hours before use.

RITUAL SUGGESTION

After a long day, wind down by sharing a cup of tea or cocktail with your significant other and give each other a sensual healing massage. Hold your hands over the massage bars after they are poured in the molds and say this affirmation: *Goddess blessed me with loving hands. Heart connection, allow me to heal and understand. Through this massage I give myself to thee. Bonded in body, and spirit so we shall be. Hug me so tight and never let go. Come on massage bars, give us that glow.*

POST-HOOKUP LIMPIA ENERGY CLEANSING SPRAY

SUGGESTED TAROT CARD: Death

Everyone has bad sex every once in a while. It is important to cleanse this energy from your aura before it lingers for too long. In Mexican brujeria we call our cleansings *limpias*, and this spray is modeled after a popular recipe. This potion is the perfect substitute for when you don't have time to smudge yourself with smoke.

YOU WILL NEED

3 fl. oz. witch hazel • 3 fl. oz. glass bottle with spray top • 20–25 drops frankincense essential oil • 6–10 drops lime essential oil • 7 drops grapefruit essential oil

TIMING

Whenever you need it

METHOD

Pour the witch hazel into your glass bottle and leave the top third for essential oils. Add each essential oil one by one and blend it until you reach your desired scent. The dominant notes in this potion should be frankincense and citrus.

RITUAL SUGGESTION

Place the bottle on your love altar, asking it to help you cleanse yourself of the energy of past lovers and hookups. Leave the bottle on the altar for three days. Whenever you anticipate a hookup, bring the spray bottle with you to cleanse yourself afterward (even if it's not a bad hookup). Spray the mixture generously on yourself, focusing on your breasts, chest, and your crown and third eye. You can spray this on your sheets after sex or add a generous amount to your laundry when you wash them. For the incantation say, *On this day I so declare, negative energy can't come near me, don't you dare. Spray, spray, spray, I let go of energy. Aura is cleansed, mind is clear. Spirit guides, spirit guides, take away my fear. I am at peace, and in charge of my body. I am pure, and this is the energy I embody.*

APHRODISIAC MEXICAN HOT CHOCOLATE

SUGGESTED TAROT CARD:
King and Queen of Cups together

Cacao is sacred in Mexico and it is said to contain the spirit of the deity *Cacahuatl (ka-ka-woo-at)*. In ancient Mexico, the cacao was drank at weddings to represent the fusion of two families. The cacao ceremonial drink is traditionally prepared with a whisk.

YOU WILL NEED

4 cups unsweetened vanilla soy, cashew, or coconut milk • Small saucepan • 4 tablespoons organic cacao powder • 1 sprinkle powdered cinnamon • 1 small pinch cayenne powder (optional) • 3 tablespoons agave, maple, simple syrup, or honey to sweeten • ¼ teaspoon pure vanilla extract • Cinnamon sugar • Whipped cream • Dark chocolate shavings

TIMING

Wintertime, when you're snowed in

METHOD

Pour the plant milk into a small saucepan over low heat. As it warms up add your dry ingredients and stir, ensuring the ingredients are incorporated evenly. Whisk in your sweetener of choice until you're happy with the taste. For extra magick, coat the rim of the mugs with cinnamon sugar, whipped cream, and sprinkle the dark chocolate shavings on top.

RITUAL SUGGESTION

This potion is particularly delightful during the cold months of the year. If you have a crush you really want to seduce, plan a date indoors, and serve them this drink. This potion also works wonders because of its warmth, which, naturally raises the body heat and will prepare the both of you for touch. These herbs are also all known aphrodisiacs, which can make you horny and increase your energy. For the incantation say, *Warm cacao, entice me and my lover. Allow me to seduce, and my lover's body uncover. Let us taste your luscious properties and connect to the divine. In bed today, we both shall shine. Take us into the world of ecstasy and let us get lost in our senses. Sacred is the space you have today invented. I thank you mama cacao, for the stamina you have presented me. Happiness is present always, and we are now so free.*

MOON SEXUAL EMPOWERMENT TEA

SUGGESTED TAROT CARD: The Moon

In magick and astrology, the Sun and Moon have traditionally been associated with masculinity and femininity. However, in my opinion, the energies are gender neutral and are contained in EVERYONE regardless of their gender identity, and therefore the tea was created to balance your sexual energy as well as help you heal from any trauma you have faced (emotionally or sexually). This tea is made from herbs that are known to support the uterus and reproductive organs, especially for people who menstruate (although it can be made and consumed by a person of any gender identity).

YOU WILL NEED
1 tablespoon lady's mantle • 1 tablespoon nettle • ⅓ cup dried raspberry leaf • ¼ cup chamomile • 2 tablespoons dried spearmint • French press, teapot with mesh strainer, or empty tea bags • Water

TIMING

Any time during a Moon cycle (it is particularly helpful to support the menstrual cycle two days before a period starts as well as during)

Combine all of the dried herbs in a French press, teapot with mesh strainer, or empty tea bags for individual portions. Boil the water and pour it over the dried herbs. Steep the tea for fifteen minutes then serve. Effects are more noticeable after prolonged use (about one week of taking this tea daily).

RITUAL SUGGESTION

Commit to thirty minutes of mindfulness in which you brew the tea, drink it, meditate, and write in your journal. For the incantation say, *I am connected to you divine Moon. Healing with you is something I can do soon. I commit to healing my higher self. Thank you for offering me this help. Today I declare and repeat, I value myself, I am not just a piece of meat. From now on I vow, in only healthy and thriving relationships I will be. Thank you motherly Moon. Now my sexual energy is so in tune.*

SOLAR SEXUAL SUPPORT TEA

SUGGESTED TAROT CARDS:
Knight of Wands and the Sun together

This Sun tea is made of herbs that support blood flow to the reproductive organs. Dandelion leaf is a plant spirit that helps prevent bladder infections, and can help prevent bloating. This tea can be made and consumed by a person of any gender since it nourishes the emotional body and is great for sexual healing.

YOU WILL NEED

1 tablespoon dried dandelion leaf • ⅓ cup loose-leaf white tea • ⅛ cup dried gingko leaf • ⅛ cup dried roses • French press, teapot with mesh strainer, or empty tea bags • Water

TIMING

Any time during a Moon cycle

METHOD

Combine all of the dried herbs in a French press, teapot with mesh strainer, or empty tea bags for individual portions. Boil the water and pour it over dried herbs. Steep the tea for fifteen minutes then serve. Effects are more noticeable after prolonged use (about one week of taking this tea daily).

RITUAL SUGGESTION

Commit to thirty minutes of mindfulness in which you brew the tea, drink it, meditate, and write in your journal. For the incantation say, *Sacred Sexual energy that is so innate, today I conjure you on this date. Divine plants in this tea, I ask that you transform me from the inside out. Blessed am I to have you in my mouth. I savor your flavors and I call upon the power of my higher self to rise. So may my magick be activated each and every try.*

CUM AND QUARTZ: A MAGICAL CRYSTAL POWERED LUBE

SUGGESTED TAROT CARD:
The Ten of Cups and the World

This personal lubricant is super-powered by crystals, made with powerful aphrodisiac and skin-healing herbs. These herbs will help increase blood flow to your sexual organs, helping you connect to your sexual power through mastur- bation. The lube contains the spirit of the hemp plant and moisturizes the intimate areas of your body.

YOU WILL NEED

2 small polished crystal quartz • 2 small polished rose quartz • 3 small polished red jasper crystals • 1 large glass jar • ½ cup roses • ¼ cup calendula • ½ cup oat tops • 2 cups hempseed oil • 1 cup coconut oil • 2 large jars

TIMING

Beginning of the New Moon (leave on the altar to charge for an entire 28 days to increase its potency)

METHOD

This potion requires a lot of patience to reach perfec- tion. Since most crystals are sensitive to high heat, and shouldn't be placed on a stove-top, use the altar-infusion method described on page 24 for this potion. Cleanse and charge your crystals, placing them in your hands and speaking your intention to them directly. When you're done, place all seven crystals in your jar. Combine all of your premeasured herbs and add in the oils. Seal the jar tightly and leave it somewhere for the oils and herbs to infuse (about three to four weeks, shaking it every three to four days), then transfer everything into a new clean jar. The potion is now ready to use.

This potion contains no essential oils, so it is safe to use on the vagina, penis, and anus. Oil can break down condoms, so I suggest you use non-latex condoms (that can't break with the use of oils) or with a fluid bonded partner. (A fluid partner is someone you have monogamous sex with. This could be a married couple or someone you trust and communicate with, otherwise use condoms.) This lubricant is also amazing for toy play and solo sex.

RITUAL SUGGESTIONS

Light a few candles and relax before you start a steamy masturbation session (or you can use the lube with a partner to encourage orgasms). This potion can also be used to lubricate yoni eggs or sex toys. To make masturbation or sexual play extra special, warm up the lube before you use it (make sure it's not too hot). The heat will create an incredible and arousing sensation that you will never forget. For the incantation say, *On this day I prepare this potion, let it set my sexual energy in motion. Spirits of the crystals and plants guide me to pleasure with my hands, help me manifest the best life and orgasms I have ever had. This spell is done and my wish will come true. Life is so good, and I'm never blue.*

CHAPTER 5

RELATIONSHIP AND MARRIAGE POTIONS

As a tarot reader I receive a lot of questions and concerns from my clients regarding the barriers they face in their love lives, most often coming from those who are married or have been in long relationships full time. Some of the most common things I'm asked to do is fidelity magick to help a partner stop cheating or magick to help bring lovers back and rekindle their passion. I think it's important to perform the magick together as a couple to help enhance and increase the love and happiness within your home and marriage! Many of these recipes also serve the purpose of bringing joy and uplifting all those who step into your home, not just your spouse or lover.

HAPPY MARRIAGE MISTLETOE POTPOURRI

SUGGESTED TAROT CARD: The Eight of Pentacles

This is a simple way to make magick a part of your everyday life! Herbal potpourri is easy to make and can be placed in all rooms of your house to promote a happy marriage and loving vibes. This potion is specifically useful when you have in-laws or family members coming to visit because it will promote love and reduce family conflict.

When collecting ingredients, make sure that you pick larger flowers and herbs since they will maintain their scent for longer.

YOU WILL NEED

1 tablespoon dried mistletoe • 1 cup dried red rose petals • ½ cup dried chrysanthemum flowers • 8 star anise pods • ½ cup cinnamon chips or small cinnamon sticks • 2 tablespoons dried juniper berries • 2 tablespoons dried hibiscus flower • 2 medium stainless-steel bowls • 1 tablespoon orris root powder • 20–30 drops patchouli essential oil • 10 drops lemon essential oil • 10 drops ylang-ylang essential oil

TIMING

Anytime

METHOD

Mix together your dried herbs in a medium stainless-steel bowl. Fluff and empower them with your hands. In a separate bowl, place your orris root powder and add the essential oils drop by drop. Mix and blend this in with your bulk herbs until you achieve your desired scent.

RITUAL SUGGESTION

Place your potpourri in a bowl or pretty glass container. Replace potpourri at the start of every Full Moon and repeat your incantation more often if the scent weakens over time. For the incantation say, *Peace is abundant in this home. My marriage (or relationship) is steady and under control. So may my higher self and my spirit guides help me. Firm is this marriage (or relationship) and strong like a tree. Conflict, conflict, go away. This home and this relationship are now declared safe. All evil, all malice it cannot stay. I chase away all negative vibration from this home. So may these loving and healing plants keep everything under divine control.*

COUPLE'S SWEETENING BODY SCRUB

SUGGESTED TAROT CARD: Knight of Swords

Sweetening magick is common when it comes to increasing love and creating special bonds between couples.

YOU WILL NEED

2 cups organic granulated or brown sugar •
2 tablespoons coffee grounds • Honey •
1–2 tablespoons organic apricot kernel or sweet almond oil • 1–2 teaspoons organic vanilla extract •
10 drops coffee essential oil (optional but superpowers the energy work) • 1 glass jar

TIMING

This is an anytime spell, but recommended that you perform it under the Full Moon for magnified effect

METHOD

Combine the dry ingredients in a bowl and mix them well. Insert the honey and distribute it evenly with your hands. Lastly, add in your oil and vanilla extract and store in a glass jar until you and your partner shower together.

Use this scrub during a steamy shower together. Apply it to your partner's body, then have them apply it to yours. Embrace each other while the hot water pours over the both of you for three to four minutes. Breathe in the aroma of each other's skin, which will smell of vanilla and coffee, and be irresistible once you perform this ritual. For the incantation say, *Sweetness is present and honored here. We share in this moment as a couple and hold each other dear. Our bond as a couple is sacred. Please help us spirit of coffee to awaken. May we embody this sweetness in our daily lives. Onwards, together always, and so we thrive.*

HONEYMOON DAY BUBBLE BATH

SUGGESTED TAROT CARD: Ten of Cups

Special occasions carry powerful energetic thresholds that can amplify the power of the magick you perform. Using this enchanted bubble-bath potion on your honeymoon will inject good energy into your marriage and prepare you both for the future. Since couples often travel for their honeymoons, I recommend bringing a bottle of this potion with you so you can spend time lovin' up on one another.

YOU WILL NEED

1 cup liquid castile soap • 2 tablespoons vegetable glycerin • ½ tablespoon honey • 7–10 drops lavender essential oil • 20–30 drops vanilla essential oil • 1 small bowl • 1 bottle with a lid

TIMING

Three to four days before your honeymoon

METHOD

Combine all of the ingredients in a small bowl. Stir them well, until the vegetable glycerin and honey are fully incorporated. Transfer the bubble bath to a bottle with a lid. Seal and let the bubble bath sit for two days.

RITUAL SUGGESTION

Draw a warm bath and light three white candles for ambiance. Pour the entire bottle into the bath and wait until it's foamy. Then, pop a bottle of champagne and pour a splash of it into your bath to celebrate the union. Bathe for fifteen to twenty minutes. (You can also save this ritual for after the honeymoon to continue your fun!) For the incantation say, *Blessed are we after marriage day. So may the passion be here to stay. We bathe together in champagne and bliss. Clanking our glasses and promising love with every kiss. Ten of Cups, I call upon your image to bring us luck and longevity. So may our new life together as partners begin and bam it's just chemistry!*

TRUST-BUILDING POWDER

SUGGESTED TAROT CARD: The Hierophant

Although I like to encourage people to be in open relationships, those who desire an extra hand with keeping their partners faithful and increasing trust can use this simple powder. The base of this powder is dried orris root, which is a plant spirit that heightens love and affection.

YOU WILL NEED

½ tablespoon powdered orris root • ½ tablespoon dried hawthorne berries • ½ tablespoon dried elderberry • ½ tablespoon arrowroot powder • Mortar and pestle (or spice grinder) • 4–5 drops jasmine essential oil

TIMING

Two days leading up to the New Moon

METHOD

Combine all dry ingredients in a mortar and pestle (or a spice grinder) and grind them to a fine powdery consistency, similar to sugar. Add the jasmine essential oil drop by drop until your desired scent is achieved. Mix everything together well.

RITUAL SUGGESTIONS

Sprinkle this powder in the four corners of your bedroom and in between your sheets. You can also use it in the drawers where you keep your underwear. If your partner does a lot of traveling, lightly sprinkle this powder into their suitcase, shoes, and socks to prevent cheating while away. (Make sure it is not noticeable.) For the incantation say, *Trusted Hierophant I call upon your powers. Help me to accomplish my intentions and desires. I wish to build trust with my partner and truly believe. I know through your guidance that lying and cheating will leave. I invite in honesty, good partnership, and hope. Thank you today, wise and old pope.*

HAPPY HOME FLOOR WASH

SUGGESTED TAROT CARD: Ten of Wands

Floor washes are incredibly useful for cleansing and blessing the space in which you live. In Mexican brujeria, it is recommended that you mop this solution from the back to front of the house while you visualize negative energy leaving your space.

YOU WILL NEED

1 dried sprig rosemary • 1 tablespoon dried lemon peel • 1 tablespoon chamomile flowers • 1 tablespoon spearmint • 1 tablespoon five finger grass (protective for the home) • 1 quart water • 1 saucepan • 1 bucket • 1 tablespoon apple cider vinegar • 3 drops cedar essential oil

TIMING

New Moon or Waxing Moon

METHOD

Add the dried herbs into the water and bring it to a boil in a saucepan. This is similar to that of making tea, but you won't be drinking any of it. Let the mixture cool down and strain out the dried herbs. Put this liquid in a bucket.

Then add in the vinegar and the essential oil drops, one by one.

RITUAL SUGGESTION

After mopping the entire house, raise your hands in a protective gesture and empower the entrance to your home with the incantation below. The herbs in this floor wash encourage peace in the home and draw in abundance. You can also use part of this floor wash to wipe down doorknobs, which can hold negative energy, especially from those who pass through your home. For the incantation say, *Ten of Wands who eliminates all difficulty. Bless my home with loving vibes and prosperity. Eliminate problems, and create harmony. This home is protected from all enemies Please seal this door against all negative energy and harmful vibration. This home is a heaven, and there is no place for frustration.*

RING BLESSING POTION

Before giving a ring to your boo, you should make sure to bless it. Rings hold the energy of those who have touched them, so blessing it could separate any wicked intention.

YOU WILL NEED

½ cup dried spikenard • ½ cup dried deer's tongue herb • 3 cups spring water • Saucepan

TIMING

The day of your anniversary or a Full Moon

METHOD

This potion is as easy as brewing tea. Place the spikenard, dried deer's tongue, and spring water in a saucepan and let it come to a boil. Let the mixture cool down and strain out all of the herbal material. Bless the water mixture by holding your hands (or wand, moving clockwise) above it while speaking your intention. The water is now sacred and programmed with your intention.

RITUAL SUGGESTION

On the day of your and your partner's anniversary, exchange rings and anoint them with this potion. Look each other in the eyes as you exchange your vows once again, and place the rings on each other's fingers like you had on your wedding day. These herbs encourage a long and happy marriage.

Another use for this potion is to give luck during a proposal. If you are the person proposing, wipe down each ring with this lucky mixture and then go in for your big moment! To attract a marriage proposal, speak in the affirmative before attempting proposal: *I am engaged to the love of my life, (insert their name) I so wish from the deepest part of my heart, to marry the lover from whom I never want to depart. Bless these rings, spirits of love. And so may this engagement happen with the blessings of those from above.*

For a ring blessing, repeat this incantation together: *Time has been kind to us as the years pass. Oh all these years have gone by fast. We honor our marriage today in this special way. Brought together by heaven and cosmos, forever to stay. We guard each other's hearts and protect these rings. Thank you spirits for giving us all that you bring. We are united, our vows we exchange. Through the grace of Goddess we embrace all challenge and change. Our marriage can overcome anything and this is our vow. Now let us commit to enjoying each other and live in the now.*

FAIRY-TALE LOVE BATH

SUGGESTED TAROT CARD: The Four of Cups

Bathing is not only good for your skin, but it is also a great time to FOCUS your energy on manifesting the right lover. Use this potion to help you visualize the lover of your dreams for a perfect fairy-tale story.

YOU WILL NEED

10 cardamom pods • 1 cup baking soda • 4 cups Epsom salt • 3 tablespoons jasmine buds • 3 tablespoon dried roses • 1 metal bowl • 20 drops vanilla essential oil • ½ tablespoon pumpkin seed oil

TIMING
Anytime

METHOD

Place all dry ingredients in a clean metal bowl and distribute them evenly with your hands. Visualize a yellow light surrounding your bath mixture. Add in the vanilla essential oil, drop by drop, and pumpkin seed oil, and blend everything together until you achieve your desired scent. The pumpkin seed oil is a key ingredient because it brings in the energy of fantasy and imagination that is associated with fairy tales.

RITUAL SUGGESTION

This ritual may seem silly, but it is inspired by Cinderella and other fairy-tale love stories. Write down a detailed love story or wedding plan while you sit in this bath for fifteen to twenty minutes. Being vulnerable and writing down your perfect love story will help you realize what you're worth! Repeat this ritual bath once a week for a month. For the incantation say, *I have dreamt of the perfect love and I will it into existence. No matter how long it takes I will be persistent. Just like fairy tale princesses, I believe in true love. May my wishes and intentions be heard from above. I set the intention to find my soul mate. Wedding, dream home, it's all possible. Just like the Four of Cups I think this is plausible. I speak this into existence every time I do this bath. Please spirit bring this love to my path.*

CHAPTER 6

HEARTBREAK AND HEALING

As I have mentioned before, every witch is tapped into their own healing powers. Healing is something that all witches practice because it connects us to nature and our soul. In my culture, and within the teachings of indigenous elders all over the world, it is believed that events like heartbreak and trauma can disconnect you from your soul, so it is extremely important to mend these wounds with magick, introspection, and especially time. Be gentle to yourself as you heal and mend. Acknowledge that no one can teach or tell you how to go through this grieving process while you reconnect to your divine self. As long as you can remember to love yourself, you will never be alone, plus you have your spirit guides to help you along the way! I wish you luck on this journey of healing and hope that the magick in the following chapter can help you finally push through the hardest of heartbreaks.

MOVE ON HEALING HERBAL SALVE

SUGGESTED TAROT CARD: Two of Wands

This balm is particularly useful to cut cords or heal from past relationships and crushes. Malachite crystals draw emotions to the surface, clear and activate the chakras, and help people break old emotional patterns.

YOU WILL NEED

INGREDIENTS FOR THE HERBAL INFUSED OIL

¼ cup dried comfrey • ¼ cup dried hyssop • ¼ cup dried motherwort • ¼ cup dried calendula • 3½ cups avocado oil

INGREDIENTS FOR THE HEALING SALVE

1 cup herbal infused oil (above) • 1 oz. beeswax or beeswax pastilles • Double boiler • 1 polished malachite crystal per salve tin • Salve tins • 5–10 drops vetiver essential oil

TIMING

The Waning Moon phase

METHOD

For the herbal infusion, use the slow cooker method mentioned on page 25. Strain out all of the plant material and set the oil aside. Combine the beeswax and herbal oil in a double boiler and warm on low heat until melted. Add about half of your beeswax mixture first and let it melt down. Check the consistency as it melts. It should be waxy rather than liquid to achieve the perfect salve. As you craft your salve, it's important to decide if you want a creamier salve with more oil and less beeswax, or a waxier salve containing more wax than oil.

Place your malachite crystals in the empty tins. Pour in the beeswax and oil mixture over the crystals. Add the vetiver plant oil (for the feeling of tranquility) as the mixture cools down. It is important to have a strong scent since it's going to help you heal through its smell. NOTE: Herbal balms are made by following an easy two-step process.

RITUAL SUGGESTION

Rub this healing balm on your heart, chest, and third eye, or use it for a healing pelvic massage, being careful not to get it too close to your genitals. For the incantation say, *I declare that I possess great strength to overcome my love wounds. Never again will love be my doom. Self love is a lesson I embrace and I learn. Attachments and fixations I am ready to burn. Oh Two of Wands, your spirit I embody. All toxic relationships are now out of my body. Hope is what's next, out into the world I go, with my new power to flex.*

DETOX BATH

SUGGESTED TAROT CARD: Five of Cups

The baths will moisturize and soothe your skin while providing you with powerful spiritual benefits. The tea tree oil and charcoal combination in this bath will remove even the heaviest of energy. This recipe will yield enough bath salts for up to two baths. Store your extra bath salt in a glass container.

YOU WILL NEED

½ tablespoon coconut oil • ⅓ cup dried rue • 1 teaspoon activated black charcoal • 2 tablespoons chamomile flowers • 3 cups Epsom salt • ⅓ cup baking soda • 1 metal bowl • 10–20 drops lemongrass essential oil • 10–15 drops tea tree oil • 1 glass container

TIMING

Anytime

METHOD

Place all dry ingredients in a clean metal bowl and distribute them evenly with your hands. Visualize a green light surrounding your bath mixture. Add essential oils, drop by drop, and blend them together with your hands until you reach your desired scent.

Take the bath salts and add them to the hot water. Bathe in the water for fifteen to twenty minutes. Repeat the bath two times a week for one month. This ritual becomes more powerful if you spend fifteen to twenty minutes writing down any of the experiences and people you want to detox from. After you finish your bath, rip up the paper you wrote on and discard it to symbolize yourself moving on. For the incantation say, *In my darkest of times I vow to never abandon my soul. I am deeply committed to healing and creating magick within this bowl. I call upon the powers of these herbs for my bath. Soon I will recover from all that is bad. Five of Cups, I honor your energy and recognize that my sadness is only temporary. Spirit Guides I believe in your ability to help me. After leaving this bath I am stronger. Now out into the world all obstacles I conquer.*

POWERFUL HEART-HEALING & HEARTBREAK-PREVENTION BALM

SUGGESTED TAROT CARD: The Hermit

Magick isn't just for when you're hurting! It can be used to prevent future heartbreak as well. This herbal salve contains powerful healing herbs, and the primary spirit healers are St. John's wort and angelica root. They are amazing guardians and can lead you through your emotional healing journey. In magick, angelica root is believed to be a guardian of women and children, and St. John's wort has pain-relieving and antidepressant qualities, which will help with boosting your mood after a breakup. Women who are taking oral contraceptives (pills) should check with their doctor before consuming St. John's wort because it can decrease the effectiveness of oral contraception. Barrier methods like condoms are highly encouraged for people using this potion. NOTE: St. John's Wort may interfere with birth control and other medications, so make sure to check with your doctor or herbalist if this is an herb you can use. It is otherwise incredibly safe to use and there is strong scientific evidence that this herb helps heal depression. This herb can also make you sun sensitive so refrain from going out into harsh sunlight when using this product or cover up with clothing.

YOU WILL NEED

INGREDIENTS FOR THE HERBAL INFUSED OIL

1 cup arnica flowers • ¼ cup angelica root •
¼ cup of calendula • ¼ cup chamomile •
¼ cup St. John's Wort (if you can't use St. John's Wort
you can omit this ingredient and the salve will still be
very healing) • 2 cups avocado oil •
1½ cups apricot seed oil or coconut oil

INGREDIENTS FOR THE HEALING BALM

1 cup herbal infused oil • 1 oz. beeswax or
beeswax pastilles • Double boiler • 1 polished rose
quartz crystal per salve tin • Salve tins • 20–40
drops lavender essential oil

TIMING

During a New Moon

METHOD

For the herbal infusion, use the slow cooker method mentioned on page 25. Strain out all of the plant material and set the oil aside. Combine the beeswax and herbal oil in a double boiler and warm on low heat until melted. Add about half of your beeswax mixture first and let it melt down. Check the consistency as it melts. It should be waxy rather than liquid to achieve the perfect salve. As you craft your salve, it's important to decide if you want a creamier salve with more oil and less beeswax, or a waxier salve containing more wax than oil.

Place your rose quartz crystals in the empty tins. Pour in the beeswax and oil mixture over the crystals. The final step is to give the salve a scent. Add in the lavender (known for its tranquil and soothing qualities) as the mixture cools down. For the salve, it is important to have a strong scent since it's going to help you heal through its smell. NOTE: Herbal balms are made by following an easy two-step process.

RITUAL SUGGESTION

This balm is made from highly protective and healing herbs. Rub this healing balm on your heart and chest, third eye, and use it to give yourself a healing pelvic massage to release sexual and romantic pain. For the incantation say,

Oh heartbreak and hurting, you are a thing of the past. On this day Spirit of the Hermit I have one thing to ask. Help me embody your wisdom and inner peace. Help me to embrace being alone, and know that my pain is to decrease. On this day I honor that I don't need a partner to feel whole. I am one with my past, present, future and my soul. Thank you divine plants for helping me heal. And so through this salve I now can feel.

RELAXATION & MEDITATION BATH

SUGGESTED TAROT CARD: Eight of Cups

When you are ready to evolve spiritually, you will have no problem moving on and relaxing. Bathe in this to reduce stress and tension related to dating.

YOU WILL NEED

4 cups Epsom salt • ½ cup baking soda • ⅛ cup dried lavender • ⅛ cup blue lotus petals • 1 metal bowl • 10–20 drops sandalwood essential oil

TIMING

Twice a week for best results (use at twilight or right before bed to encourage mindful sleeping and dreaming)

METHOD

Place all dry ingredients in a clean metal bowl and distribute the ingredients evenly with your hands. Visualize a purple light surrounding your bath mixture. Add essential oils, drop by drop, and blend them together until you reach your desired scent.

RITUAL SUGGESTION

Add the bath salts to hot water and bathe yourself for fifteen to twenty minutes. Repeat the bath twice per week for one month. Say this incantation over your bath mix before getting in: *Hot water, hot water, I speak to thee. I brew this potion with the intention to relax and enjoy serenity. As I sit in this bath I let myself release all tension and problems. My sacred bath time is where I come to feel awesome. I quiet my mind. I search, I search, I go within and find. Deep deep I go, knowing my true self and finding my flow.*

CHAPTER 7

ZODIAC POTIONS

BASIC ASTROLOGY FOR LOVE
AND SEX MAGICK

Astrology is one of the most important tools in witchcraft and every beginner witch should do their best to at least know the basics.

There are twelve commonly recognized zodiac signs in the night sky, and they are each represented by a constellation. They are also all assigned a ruling planet and element (fire, water, air, earth). The Sun consistently moves through the night sky and each constellation. When someone asks you for your zodiac sign, they are actually asking about which constellation the Sun was under when you were born. The rest of the planets also influence your world and personality, but for the sake of this book, we will focus on Sun sign magick. The Sun represents our personality, our conscious self, and major parts of our identity. The following is a useful guide to help you remember key characteristics of each sign and their best romantic astrological matches. The following astrological dates are identified on the popular website "Astrostyle" by the Astro Twins.

Aries (Mar 21–Apr 19)

Aries is a fire sign ruled by the planet Mars. It is typically associated with the positive traits of leadership, dominance, independence, originality, and courage. The negative characteristics of Aries include impulsiveness, anger, and impatience. The best love matches for Aries are said to be Sagittarius, Gemini, and Leo.

Taurus (Apr 20–May 20)

Taurus is an Earth sign ruled by the planet Venus. It is typically associated with the positive characteristics of reliability, strength, stability, sensuality, and love of pleasure. The negative characteristics of Taurus include stubbornness, slowness, excessive spending, and obsession with the material world. The best love matches for Taurus are said to be Cancer and Pisces.

Gemini (May 21–Jun 20)

Gemini is an Air sign ruled by Mercury. It is typically associated with the positive characteristics of intelligence, good humor, reliability, adaptability, quick-wittedness, and a great ability to communicate. The negative characteristics of Gemini include temperament issues and nervousness. The best love matches for Gemini are said to be Libra and Aquarius.

Cancer (June 21–July 22)

Cancer is a water sign ruled by the Moon. It is typically associated with the positive characteristics of femininity, receptiveness, intuition, and a maternal nature. The negative characteristics of Cancer include passiveness and being overly emotional. The best love matches for Cancer are said to be Taurus, Scorpio, and Virgo.

Leo (July 23–Aug 22)

Leo is a fire sign ruled by the Sun. It is typically associated with the positive characteristics of courage, leadership, loyalty, confidence, and self-assurance. The negative characteristics associated with Leo are excessive attention-seeking, inflexibility, and laziness. The best love matches for Leo are Gemini, Aries, and Sagittarius.

Virgo (Aug 23–Sep 22)

Virgo is an Earth Sign ruled by the planet Mercury. It is typically associated with the positive characteristics of femininity, helpfulness, cleanliness, attractiveness, and a strong work ethic. The negative characteristics associated with Virgo are shyness, nervousness, and excessive self-criticism. The best love matches for Virgo are Cancer, Scorpio, and Capricorn.

Libra (Sep 23–Oct 22)

Libra is an air sign ruled by the planet Venus. It is typically associated with the positive characteristics of justice, balance, love, charm, optimism, and romance. The negative characteristics associated with Libra are a detached nature, having a tendency to want to please others, and narcissism. The best love matches for Libra are Gemini, Sagittarius, and Aquarius.

Scorpio (Oct 23–Nov 21)

Scorpio is a water sign ruled by Mars and Pluto. Scorpio is typically associated with the positive characteristics of intuition, renewal, sexiness, and a strong will. The negative characteristics associated with Scorpio are excessive secrecy, vindictiveness, and jealousy. The best love matches for Scorpio are Cancer and Pisces.

Sagittarius (Nov 22–Dec 21)

Sagittarius is a fire sign ruled by Jupiter. Sagittarius is typically associated with the positive characteristics of adventure, humor, supportiveness, optimism, and freedom. The negative characteristics associated with Sagittarius are frankness, procrastination, sarcasm, and a harsh sense of humor. The strongest love matches for Sagittarius are Aries, Leo, and Libra.

Capricorn (Dec 22–Jan 19)

Capricorn is an Earth sign ruled by Saturn. Capricorn is typically associated with the positive characteristics of persistence, prestige and honor, practicality, and strength. The negative characteristics associated with Capricorn are stoicism, pessimism, and being too work-driven. The strongest love matches for Capricorn are Virgo and Scorpio.

Aquarius (Jan 20–Feb 18)

Aquarius is an air sign ruled by the planets Saturn and Uranus. Aquarius is typically associated with the positive characteristics of being independent, worldly, friendly, intellectual, and forward-thinking. The negative characteristics associated with Aquarius are being a bit chaotic, and sometimes cold and detached. The strongest love matches for Aquarius are Sagittarius, Gemini, and Libra.

Pisces (Feb 19–Mar 20)

Pisces is a water sign ruled by Neptune. Pisces is typically associated with the positive characteristics of creativity, musicianship, emotional intelligence, and introspectiveness. The negative characteristics associated with Pisces are being self-sacrificing and too emotionally sensitive. The strongest love matches for Pisces are Scorpio, Capricorn, and Cancer.

ZODIAC POTIONS

Astrology can really help you understand and master yourself. Although your personality contains multiple characteristics, knowing your strengths and weaknesses through the lens of astrology can help you become a better person and find a partner suited for you.

Perfume magick can be traced back to ancient times, and it can work wonders on your power of attraction. These zodiac potions are all uniquely formulated perfumes designed to accentuate your personality and help you attract love by working with the magick of your astrological sign. Astrology is key to human existence. Once you master your zodiac sign, you master yourself.

For the zodiac potions, it is important to pay extra

attention to how YOU feel about the suggested scent combinations. The amount of essential oil you use in these potions may seem like a lot, but it will help the scent last longer. All the potions contain one secret ingredient: licorice root, which has incredible love-attracting properties.

TIMING

These potions can be created at any point in time, but if you want to maximize their effort, you can create them during the Moon phase of that sign. The Moon moves around the zodiac much faster than the Sun, and so it is useful to track its movements in the sky as well. Typically she spends a brief 2–3 days in each sign and you can easily look this up online. If you feel called to make this potion without thinking about the astrological placement of the Moon or the Sun then that is also fine. None of these potions will have tarot cards, as they are powerful archetypes on their own.

ARIES

Avocado seed oil • 1 small roller bottle • 2 licorice
root slices, or a small pinch licorice root chips •
12 drops bergamot essential oil • 5 drops ginger
essential oil • 2–3 drops basil essential oil

METHOD

Add the avocado seed oil as a base to a small roller
bottle. Then place one to two licorice root slices or chips
into the roll-on bottle. Carefully add the suggested amount
of essential oils into the bottle. It is best to fill the bottle
halfway, add the essential oils, then top off the bottle with
carrier oil to finish.

The scent should give off soft notes of basil and ginger,
and high notes of bergamot. This scent will magnify your
natural sexual energy.

RITUAL SUGGESTION

Whisper the following incantation over your potion when
it's finished and draw the planetary symbol of Mars on
your bottle. Wear this potion every day. For the incantation say, *Fuego, Fuego, light within. I am Aries, lord
of fire, passion is in my skin. I'm a lover, I'm a young*

soul. Light of Aries help me reach my goals. Aries lord of fire, ignite within me the passion of your sign. I call upon stamina, creativity and leadership so divine. So may I embody these qualities and just know that Aries energy ignites within my soul.

TAURUS

YOU WILL NEED

Avocado seed oil • 1 small roller bottle • 2 licorice root slices, or a pinch licorice root chips • 10 drops rose essential oil • 8–10 drops blood orange essential oil • 12 drops vanilla essential oil • 3–4 pieces dried orange peels

METHOD

Add the avocado seed oil as a base to a small roller bottle, then place one to two slices of licorice root into the roll-on bottle. Carefully add the suggested amount of essential oils into the bottle. Add crushed and empowered herbs into the roll-on bottle. Top off the bottle with carrier oil to finish and shake well to incorporate plant materials.

Whisper the following incantation over your potion when it's finished and draw the planetary symbol of Venus on your bottle. Wear this potion every day. For the incantation say, *I am Taurus and in my strength I stand. Unshakeable, secure of self and abundant I am. Everywhere I go, people admire my beauty. Embodying Venus energy is my duty. Even though sometimes I am misunderstood, in my Earth energy I am wise and sacred like wood. So may I embody these qualities and just know that Taurus energy runs within my soul.*

GEMINI

YOU WILL NEED

Avocado seed oil • 1 small roller bottle • 2 licorice root slices, or a small pinch licorice root chips • 12 drops eucalyptus essential oil • 8 drops lavender essential oil • Dried chamomile flowers

METHOD

Add the avocado seed oil as a base to a small roller bottle. Then place one to two slices of licorice root into the roll-on bottle. Carefully add the suggested amount of essential oils into the bottle. Add crushed and empowered herbs into the roll-on bottle. Top off the bottle with carrier oil to finish and shake well to incorporate plant materials.

RITUAL SUGGESTION

Whisper the following incantation over your potion when it's finished and draw the planetary symbol of Mercury on your bottle. Wear this potion every day. For the incantation say, *So blessed was I upon birth, that my energy was divided in two. Gemini I was born, and this is what I do. I am soft and feminine like music from a flute. I am duality, I am a shifter, I am what is true. Air is pure it helps us breathe. Gemini energy is what I need. I call upon intelligence, wit and honesty and I declare these are my greatest qualities. So may I embody these qualities and just know that Gemini energy flows within my soul.*

CANCER

YOU WILL NEED

Avocado seed oil • 1 small roller bottle •
2 licorice slices, or a small pinch licorice root
chips • 10 drops neroli essential oil • 10 drops
mandarin essential oil • 5 drops jasmine essential
oil • Dried jasmine buds

METHOD

Add the avocado seed oil as a base to a small roller
bottle. Then place one to two slices of licorice root into
the roll-on bottle. Carefully add the suggested amount of
essential oils into the bottle. Add crushed and empowered
herbs into the roll-on bottle. Top off the bottle with carrier
oil to finish and shake well to incorporate plant materials.

RITUAL SUGGESTION

Whisper the following incantation over your potion when
it's finished and draw the planetary symbol of the Moon
on your bottle. Wear this potion every day. For the incantation say, *I am Cancer, and you may not hear me roar.
I am quiet energy, but boy do I know how to soar. I am
psychic, I can see into other realms. Cancer energy
doesn't overwhelm. I am sea, I am Moon, I am peace.
I am also everything in between. My gifts are intuition,*

love and motherly energy. And so I move through life always cleverly. So may I embody these qualities and just know that Cancer energy flows within my soul.

LEO

YOU WILL NEED

Avocado seed oil • 1 small roller bottle • 2 licorice root slices, or a small pinch licorice root chips • 15–25 drops cedar essential oil • 1–2 small calendula flowers

METHOD

Add the avocado seed oil as a base to a small roller bottle. Then place one to two slices of licorice root into the roll-on bottle. Carefully add the suggested amount of essential oil into the bottle. Add crushed and empowered herbs into the roll-on bottle. Top off the bottle with carrier oil to finish and shake well to incorporate plant materials.

RITUAL SUGGESTION

Whisper the following incantation over your potion when it's finished and draw the planetary symbol of the Sun on your bottle. Wear this potion every day. For the incantation say, *Mighty so I am. Great Leo unconfined. Look inside my soul, and loyalty you will find. I am proud and at times attention I demand. Nothing stops me, I'm a Leo and I know who I am. I am ruled by the Sun, who sustains us all. Hanging out with me will always be a ball. I am generous, abundant and rich and my qualities will always leave you feeling bewitched. So may I embody these characteristics and just know that Leo energy burns within my soul.*

VIRGO

YOU WILL NEED

Avocado seed oil • 1 small roller bottle • 2 licorice root slices, or a small pinch licorice root chips • 12 drops bergamot essential oil • 7–8 drops frankincense essential oil • 6 drops ylang-ylang essential oil • Dried green tea leaves

METHOD

Add the avocado seed oil as a base to a small roller bottle. Then place one to two slices of licorice root into the roll-on bottle. Carefully add the suggested amount of essential oils into the bottle. Add crushed and empowered herbs into the roll-on bottle. Top off the bottle with carrier oil to finish and shake well to incorporate plant materials.

RITUAL SUGGESTION

Whisper the following incantation over your potion when it's finished and draw the planetary symbol of Mercury on your bottle. Wear this potion every day. For the incantation say, *I'm a Virgo and I don't speak, I sing. My voice is spirit, Hermes is my king. Communication is my strength, and near perfection is my power. I am delicate like one of the most beautiful flowers. I am organized, calculated, and I know how to listen. I'm a great lover, watch me shine I glisten. I am Earth, diamond dust, and bones alike. Every bit of me is oh so incredibly alive. I am magick, I am helpful, I am medicine. I am stars and hope and it is evident in my skin. So may I embody these qualities and just know that Virgo energy runs within my soul.*

LIBRA

Avocado seed oil • 1 small roller bottle • 2 licorice
root slices, or a small pinch licorice root chips •
15–25 drops vanilla essential oil • 10 drops sweet
orange essential oil • 1 vanilla bean • 3–4 cinnamon
bark chips • 1 whole clove of spice (not garlic) •
1 small pinch dried roses

METHOD

Add the avocado seed oil as a base to a small roller
bottle. Then place one to two slices of licorice root into
the roll-on bottle. Carefully add the suggested amount of
essential oils into the bottle. Add crushed and empowered herbs into the roll-on bottle. Top off the bottle with
carrier oil to finish and shake well to incorporate plant
materials.

RITUAL SUGGESTION

Whisper the following incantation over your potion
when it's finished and draw the planetary symbol of
Venus on your bottle. Wear this potion every day. For
the incantation say, *I am Libra, represented by the
scales. No task is ever too hard, if I am determined*

I will never fail. Venus rules me so I can't help but be glamorous. I am loving, amorous, relationship obsessed and a perfect lifelong partner. I walk with sexual power and I'm not afraid. Goddess knew exactly what she made. I am Libra, walking in such power. When I love myself my spirit is as tall as a tower. When I'm tune with exactly who I am, Libra energy is at its best. I'm all heart just beating out my chest.

SCORPIO

YOU WILL NEED

Avocado seed oil • 1 small roller bottle • 2 licorice root slices, or a small pinch licorice root chips • 10–12 drops coffee essential oil • 1 small ginseng root (sliced or crushed if necessary) • 1 pinch dried mullein flowers

METHOD

Add the avocado seed oil as a base to a small roller bottle. Then place one to two slices of licorice root into the roll-on bottle. Carefully add the suggested amount of essential oil into the bottle. Add crushed and empowered herbs into the roll-on bottle. Top off the bottle with carrier oil to finish and shake well to incorporate plant materials.

Whisper the following incantation over your potion when it's finished and draw the planetary symbols of Mars and Pluto on your bottle. Wear this potion every day. For the incantation say, *I am Scorpio I may sometimes be mis-understood. Secrets and silence is somewhere I feel good. But when I love, I truly give it all. I'm a protector and I'll never make you feel small. People know me to be a master of pleasure. I embody this my love making is a hidden treasure. I am also drawn to the dark and the mystic. When I am really in tune with myself I am even artistic. I'm a Scorpio and I may sting. But truly love me, and I'll make your heart sing.*

SAGITTARIUS

Avocado seed oil • 1 small roller bottle • 2 licorice
root slices, or a small pinch licorice root chips •
10 drops grapefruit essential oil • 1 pinch dried
hyssop flowers

METHOD

Add the avocado seed oil as a base to a small roller
bottle. Then place one to two slices of licorice root into
the roll-on bottle. Carefully add the suggested amount of
essential oil into the bottle. Add crushed and empowered
herbs into the roll-on bottle. Top off the bottle with carrier
oil to finish and shake well to incorporate plant materials.

RITUAL SUGGESTION

Whisper the following incantation over your potion when
it's finished and draw the planetary symbol of Jupiter on
your bottle. Wear this potion every day. For the incantation say, *I'm a Sagittarius, and adventure is the lan-
guage I speak. I'm a centaur, and my soul is not weak.
I am drawn to the realms of pleasure. Life of the party
way beyond measure. Now I'm not all optimism, I am
also real. If you love me, with my centaur medicine I*

CAPRICORN

YOU WILL NEED

Avocado seed oil • 1 small roller bottle • 2 licorice root slices, or a small pinch licorice root chips • 20 drops patchouli essential oil • 4–5 drops ginger essential oil • 12 drops lemongrass essential oil • 1 pinch dried mullein

METHOD

Add the avocado seed oil as a base to a small roller bottle. Then place one to two slices of licorice root into the roll-on bottle. Carefully add the suggested amount of essential oils into the bottle. Add crushed and empowered herbs into the roll-on bottle. Top off the bottle with carrier oil to finish and shake well to incorporate plant materials.

Whisper the following incantation over your potion when it's finished and draw the planetary symbol of Saturn on your bottle. Wear this potion every day. For the incantation say, *I am Capricorn, the mighty Earth fuels the person I am. Steady, responsible and Boss moves so impressive I'll make you say damn! When I love, I truly help you rise. Capricorn energy is Saturnian and wise. I give good advice and I can say plenty. Invite me into your space and you will always feel ready. I know my strengths, and my weaknesses I fix. I am Capricorn, I never play tricks. Those who embrace me will never be alone. I am Capricorn, my partners and I will sit on a throne.*

AQUARIUS

YOU WILL NEED
Avocado seed oil • 1 small roller bottle •
2 licorice root slices, or a small pinch licorice root chips • 10 drops lime essential oil • 8 drops frankincense essential oil • 1 tablespoon dried roses • 1 tablespoon dried holy basil

METHOD

Add the avocado seed oil as a base to a small roller bottle. Then place one to two slices of licorice root into the roll-on bottle. Carefully add the suggested amount of essential oils into the bottle. Add crushed and empowered herbs into the roll-on bottle. Top off the bottle with carrier oil to finish and shake well to incorporate plant materials.

RITUAL SUGGESTION

Whisper the following incantation over your potion when it's finished and draw the planetary symbols of Uranus and Saturn on your bottle. Wear this potion everyday. For the incantation say, *I am Aquarius lord of the different path. My gifts of uniqueness are never a fad. The type of love I give can make you transcend. I'm Uranian, I'm made of stardust, the perfect blend. I take pride in my intelligence, individualism, and futuristic mindset. I'm transparent and honest, so what you see is what you get. I am Aquarius if you choose to accept, I promise you that off your feet you'll be swept. Jump on my spaceship and hold my hand. Dancing, playing, effortless, feeling like we don't belong in this land. I am Aquarius, I'm proud of who I am and I'm*

PISCES

YOU WILL NEED

Avocado seed oil • 1 small roller bottle •
2 licorice root slices, or a small pinch licorice
root chips • 8 drops clary sage essential oil • 12
drops lavender essential oil • 7–8 drops lemongrass
essential oil • One or two blue lotus flowers

METHOD

Add the avocado seed oil as a base to a small roller bottle. Then place one to two slices of licorice root into the roll-on bottle. Carefully add the suggested amount of essential oils into the bottle. Add crushed and empowered herbs into the roll-on bottle. Top off the bottle with carrier oil to finish and shake well to incorporate plant materials.

Whisper the following incantation over your potion when it's finished and draw the planetary symbol of Neptune on your bottle. Wear this potion everyday. For the incantation say, *I am Pisces, ruled by mighty Neptune. Musical, poetic and obsessed with the Moon. Many call me weak, but emotion is my strength. I can handle anything, no matter the length. I am ruled by the water, so I'm an easy flow. I speak to the spirits, they always let me know. I am intuitive, and nothing gets past me. I am Pisces, and low-key in bed, also a little bit nasty. Love me for life, and you will never be alone. I am Pisces shadow, magick, and bone. I'll listen, I'll love. I'll fill you with compassion. Come home to me and you'll never lack passion.*

HEARST
books

COSMOPOLITAN and COSMO are registered trademarks
and the distinctive Hearst Books logo is a trademark of
Hearst Communications, Inc.

© 2019 Hearst Communications, Inc.

ISBN 978-1-61837-306-9

Distributed in Canada by Sterling Publishing Co., Inc.
c/o Canadian Manda Group, 664 Annette Street
Toronto, Ontario M6S 2C8, Canada
Distributed in Australia by NewSouth Books
University of New South Wales, Sydney, NSW 2052, Australia

For information about custom editions, special sales, and premium
and corporate purchases, please contact Sterling Special Sales at
800-805-5489 or specialsales@sterlingpublishing.com.

Manufactured in Canada

2 4 6 8 10 9 7 5 3 1

sterlingpublishing.com

cosmopolitan.com

Cover design by Elizabeth Mihaltse Lindy
Interior design by Nancy Singer
Illustrations: DEPOSIT PHOTOS: DariaVolyanskaya, 119; FREEPIK: 28;
Natkacheva 71; All others SHUTTERSTOCK: Lena Nikolaeva, except
Karnoff (border design throughout); MicroOne 143